CW00758798

Cacti and Succulents

The Plant Rescuer

Sarah Gerrard-Jones

Cacti and Succulents

On-point advice to keep your plants looking sharp

Contents

Introduction

Cacti and succulents are among the most captivating plants in the world. Having evolved over millions of years to adapt to extreme landscapes, their bizarre shapes and extraordinary ability to survive against the odds have made them some of nature's most remarkable and desirable creations. From the statuesque saguaro to the jewel-like conophytum, their diverse appearance is as vast and varied as the environments they inhabit.

It was during a holiday to California that I first discovered a passion for cacti and succulents. We stayed in the Joshua Tree National Park, and for someone used to Britain's lush green landscape, venturing into the desert and walking among the towering succulents felt otherworldly. After that, we took a trip to the Getty Museum in LA, where on the rooftop we found the Cactus Garden, which looks out over the sprawling city. Predominantly planted with giant golden barrel cacti, the garden functions as a piece of living art. I was smitten. On the plane home, I knew I wanted to start my own collection of cacti and succulents, and immediately set about finding interesting specimens.

For decades I've been a lover of houseplants, with a particular fondness for rescuing ones that aren't doing well. It was while searching for plants to salvage that I saw an advert for an old cactus that was looking for a new home – a hefty 1.2-metre (4ft), multi-stemmed, 20-year-old *Cleistocactus strausii*. This white, hairy plant was the most extraordinary I'd ever seen, and so my obsession with cacti and succulents was born.

For generations, scientists, botanists, and hobbyists have been enchanted by these curious plants, writing many books on the subject. However, a lot of the information available – though invaluable – is often inaccessible to novice growers; with scientific language that can be intimidating. There is very little out there that bridges the gap between oversimplified misinformation and the juicy good stuff, and it is exactly that bridge I hope to provide.

The variety of habitats in which succulent plants grow means there are species suitable for most indoor and outdoor spaces. Some can be grown outside, unperturbed by frost and snow, and – contrary to popular belief – many will thrive in a bathroom. Understanding their native habitats will help you choose the right plant for the right place, as well as grasp the nuances of how to care for them. In this book I've included detailed information and guidance on over 150 such species, whatever your space and level of expertise.

You don't need a degree in horticulture to grow cacti and succulents successfully. All you need is an interest and willingness to learn from both failures and successes. Whether you're an experienced enthusiast or you've just picked one up at your local shop, this book will provide insight into the captivating world of growing some of the most extraordinary plants on the planet, encompassing the rich diversity of their native habitats and their care and cultivation. You'll meet experienced growers, be amazed by some of the best collections worldwide, and discover top tips for nurturing your own thriving collection, indoors and out.

Get to Know

Understanding succulence

Before the term "succulent" was used in a botanical sense, its definition (usually used to describe food) was simply "tender and juicy". It's possible that a lot of people don't stop to consider the simplicity of a name, but in this case, it is that straightforward. Succulent plants are so-called because they are fat and juicy! It's when we start to wonder why they have evolved to be so physiologically different from other plants that we get to the really interesting information.

The phenomenon of succulence is one of the most impressive instances of evolution in the plant kingdom. This unique adaptation to environmentally stressful conditions has created some of the world's most bizarre, spectacular, and covetable plants. To me, there is something mystical and otherworldly about how these plants adapt and grow, expanding, twisting, flattening, and distorting themselves in the pursuit of survival in the most challenging environments.

The first mention in scientific writing was in 1619 by Johann Bauhin, who described succulent plants as "thick-leaved and juicy herbs". However, because there haven't been any fossilized remains found, it is almost impossible to date the occurrence of plant succulence. An arid environment, it seems, isn't as conducive to fossil creation as lakes, flood plains, and oceans; therefore, the exact origins remain mysterious. Studies have deduced that the origins of succulence could date back as far as 35 million years ago. Theories such as a global period millions of years ago marked by cooling and increased aridity, possibly with lowered atmospheric carbon dioxide levels, help us understand the significant environmental impact, which gave succulent species an advantage in a wide range of ecological niches.

Most succulents – apart from cacti, which often have spines instead (top) – have thick, juicy leaves, often with a waxy coating to help retain moisture (above).

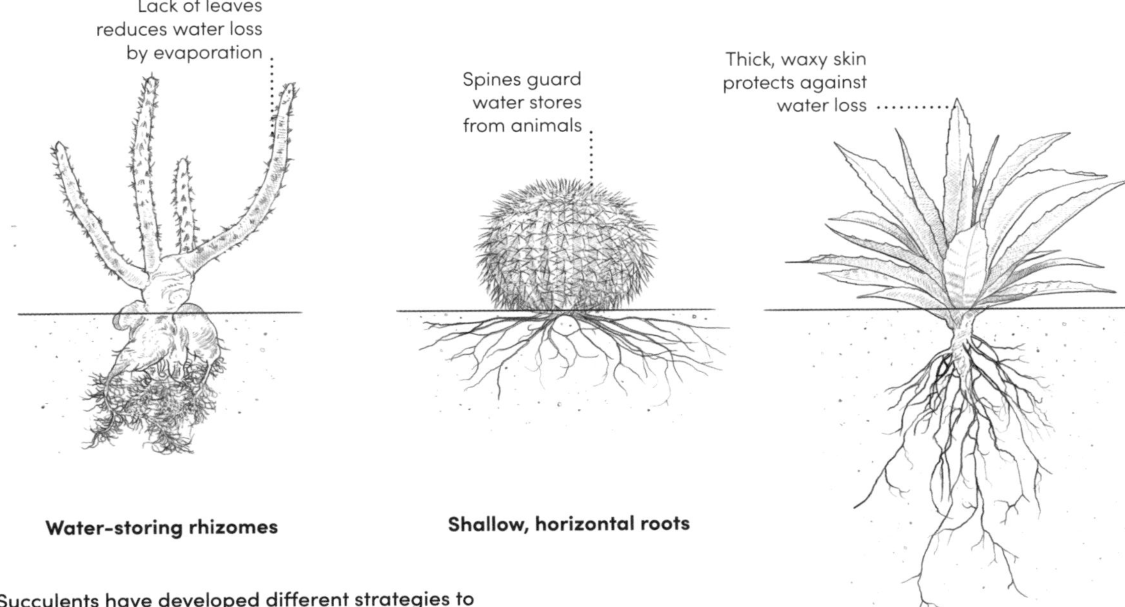

Succulents have developed different strategies to access water: some store water in tubers; some have spreading shallow roots to absorb surface water; others access the water table with deep tap roots.

Despite looking like one, this African *Euphorbia* isn't a cactus.

Convergent evolution

All cacti (except one species of *Rhipsalis*; see page 166) are native to the Americas. Cacti have since been introduced to many other places around the world, but they all come from the Americas. Why, then, do some members of the *Euphorbia* genus (see page 206), which bear such a remarkable resemblance to cacti, come from South Africa? Succulence is an example of a phenomenon known as convergent evolution. Convergent evolution is when organisms from different evolutionary lineages develop similar adaptations or traits when faced with similar environmental challenges. Despite hailing from different continents, North American cacti and African *Euphorbia* both developed similar forms. They both decided to do away with leaves, grow thick, succulent stems to store water, and add some spines for protection. The end result was plants from two different families, from two different continents, that look almost identical.

What are succulent plants?

Water is essential for the survival and growth of all vegetation, including succulent plants, which have mastered the issue of how to economize it in times of drought, but not all plants are as succulent as others. There are varying degrees of succulence, with some species, depending on their environment, being highly succulent while others store water to a lesser degree. Classifying plants into succulent and non-succulent poses several challenges, owing to the lack of clear criteria. The best definition I've come across is by D.J. von Willert in his book *Life Strategies of Succulents in Deserts* (1990), in which he describes these defining features: "A succulent is a plant possessing at least one succulent tissue. A succulent tissue is a living tissue that, besides possible other tasks, serves and guarantees an at least temporary storage of utilisable water, which makes the plant temporarily independent from external water supply, when soil water conditions have deteriorated such that the root is no longer able to provide the necessary water from the soil."

An extraordinary variety of plants meet these criteria. In total, succulence has been recorded in up to 13,000 species across more than 80 plant families, including the largest, *Cactaceae* (cactus family). However, succulence is often seen in combination with other adaptations, such as a shallow root system to rapidly absorb rainwater, a waxy coating on the leaves to inhibit water loss, and the most fascinating adaptation known as Crassulacean acid metabolism.

***Cactaceae* is the largest family of succulents. Other succulent plants come from over 80 different families.**

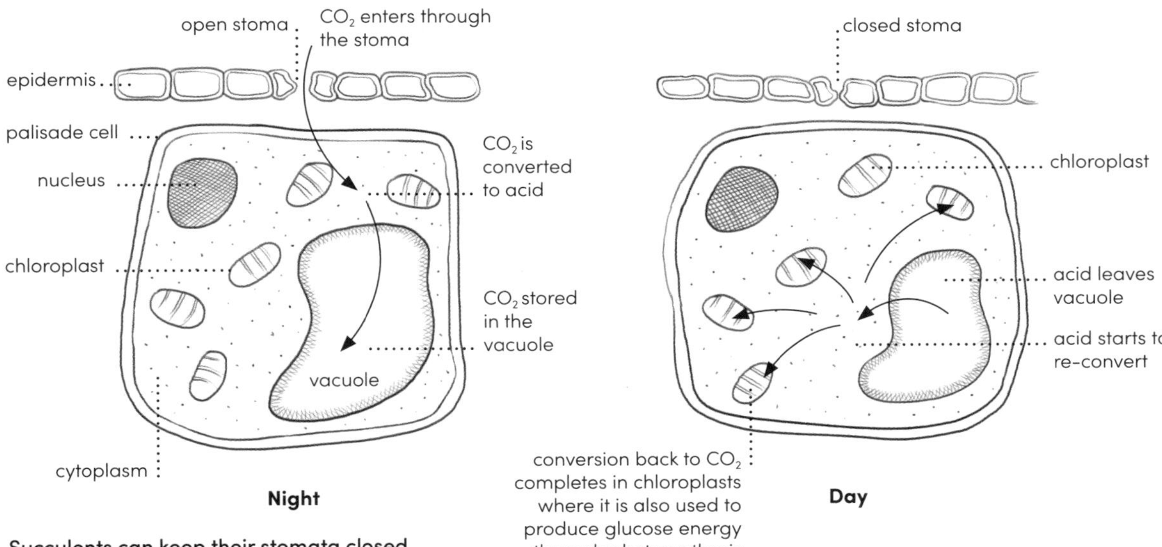

Succulents can keep their stomata closed during the day to conserve water, while still performing photosynthesis using stored carbon dioxide. This clever adaptation is known as Crassulacean acid metabolism.

Crassulacean acid metabolism

Photosynthesis is a complex process performed by all plants, the outcome of which is the same – the creation of glucose, which feeds the plant with the energy it needs to grow. However, not all plants perform the process in the same way, and this is because of differences in their habitat. All plants absorb carbon dioxide through tiny mouth-like holes on their leaves called stomata; these stomatal movements control carbon dioxide uptake and water loss through transpiration (see overleaf). During the day, most non-succulent plants open their stomata for carbon dioxide absorption, which also allows water to evaporate. Plants growing in hot places lose water through transpiration faster than those in cooler climates. This isn't a problem for plants with reliable access to water, but for succulent plants living in harsh habitats, the opening of stomata during the day causes a dilemma. The plant needs to absorb carbon dioxide but conserve water. The solution is an adaptation called Crassulacean acid metabolism (CAM). Unlike most plants that perform photosynthesis during the day, CAM plants can choose to keep their stomata closed during the day and open them at night when temperatures are cooler. The stomata absorb carbon dioxide at night, then convert it into acids and store it within the plant until daylight. As the sun rises, the stomata close, and the acids are broken down, converted into carbon dioxide, and used for photosynthesis.

Did you know?

In times of abundant water some cacti and succulents will function as "normal" plants, opening their stomata during the day and only switching to CAM when water becomes scarce.

From leaf to spine

Leaves are a vital part of most plants; they contain chlorophyll to capture sunlight for photosynthesis and stomata, which play a crucial role in transpiration.

Transpiration pull is the force that helps draw water up from the roots to the leaves. Some of this water is used for photosynthesis, and the rest is released into the atmosphere through the tiny mouth-like stomata. Considering that the average number of stomata is about 300 per square millimetre of leaf surface, you can see why transpiration is problematic for plants that need to conserve as much water as possible. To solve this, cacti modified their leaves into spines and transferred the role of capturing sunlight to the stem.

Types of spine and their functions

Spines, like leaves, perform multiple functions to ensure the plant's survival. One of their primary functions is defence against herbivores chomping into them. Another function is that they offer protection from extreme temperatures, providing both insulation from the cold and shade from the sun. Studies have shown that some spines are used to direct water into the plant, acting almost as roots.

Spines grow from an axillary bud known as an areole. In most cases, two forms of spines grow – the central spine from the centre of the areole and radial spines, which grow around the circumference. The central spines, usually strong and often colourful, act as a deterrent to grazers. In contrast, radial spines tend to be thin, white, and more flexible. White spines help to reflect sunlight away from the plant, lowering

Spines and thorns come in many shapes, sizes, and colours and have multiple functions.

the risk of harm from the sun. Species of *Opuntia* possess hair-like spines called glochids, which, although only a few millimetres in length, are a good deterrent. The short, thin spines detach easily and possess fine barbs, which make them difficult to remove. Take extra care when around *Opuntia*. One false move, and you'll be wearing glochids for the next few weeks.

The spineless ones

Some cacti are spineless or nearly so. *Lophophora williamsii* has trichomes (epidermal "hair") but no spines. It uses a chemical defence, producing a bitter, toxic substance called mescaline to protect itself from animals. Epiphytic cacti are nearly all spineless as their habitats, high up in tree branches, are mostly inaccessible to predators.

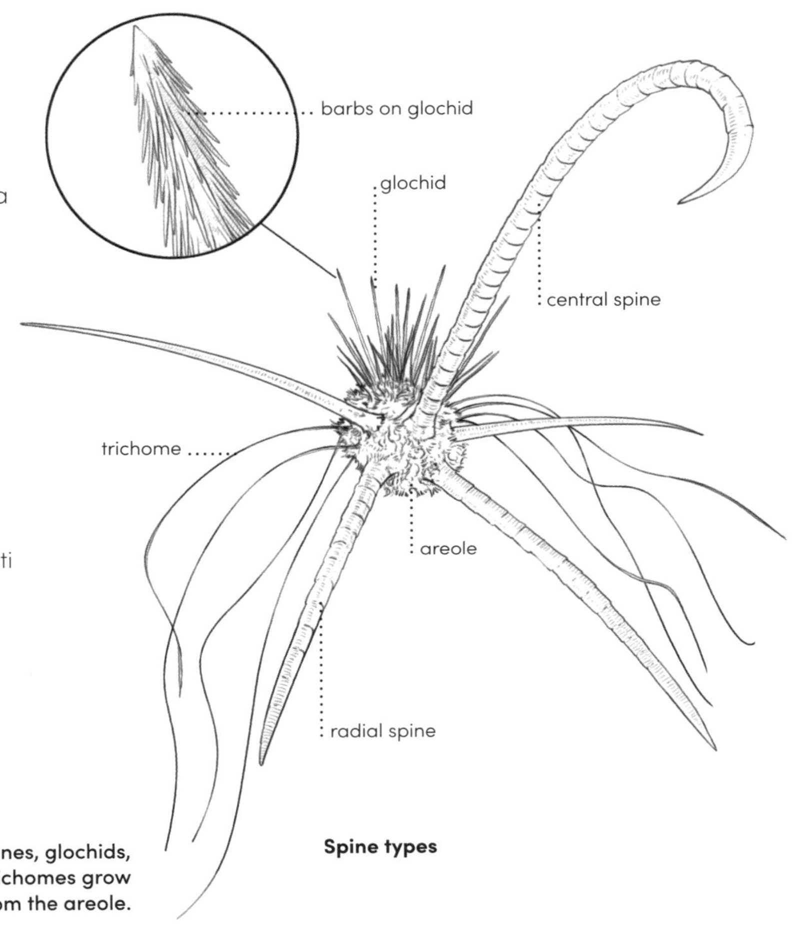

Spine types

Spines, glochids, and trichomes grow from the areole.

Fog collectors

Spines can also function as water harvesters. Some plants, such as *Espostoa lanata*, have a dense covering of white, woolly, hair-like spines, which absorb daily ocean mists, combined with central spines that point downwards to ensure that the condensed droplets of water fall directly on the soil surface, just above the shallow roots. In the Atacama Desert, the driest place on earth, *Copiapoa cinerea* var. *haseltoniana* harvests moisture from the fog on specialized spines, which condenses and rolls downwards, where it is absorbed into the areoles and into the stem of the plant.

Cactus anatomy

Want to be more confident in your cactus prowess? Let's start with the main anatomical parts of a cactus.

Cacti have adapted to survive periods of drought. Most don't have leaves but instead have spines that help to provide shade and deter predators. Their thick, water-filled stems have stomata, which can close in the heat of the day to minimize transpiration, then open at night when temperatures are cooler.

Cladode A flattened stem resembling and functioning as a leaf.

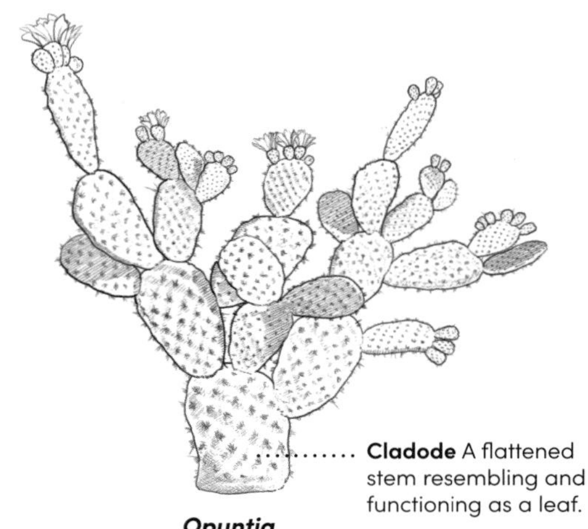

Opuntia

Stomata close up

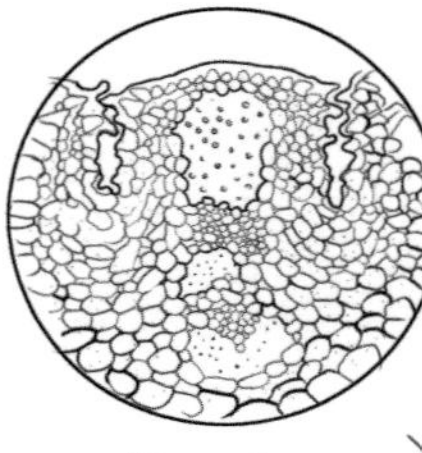

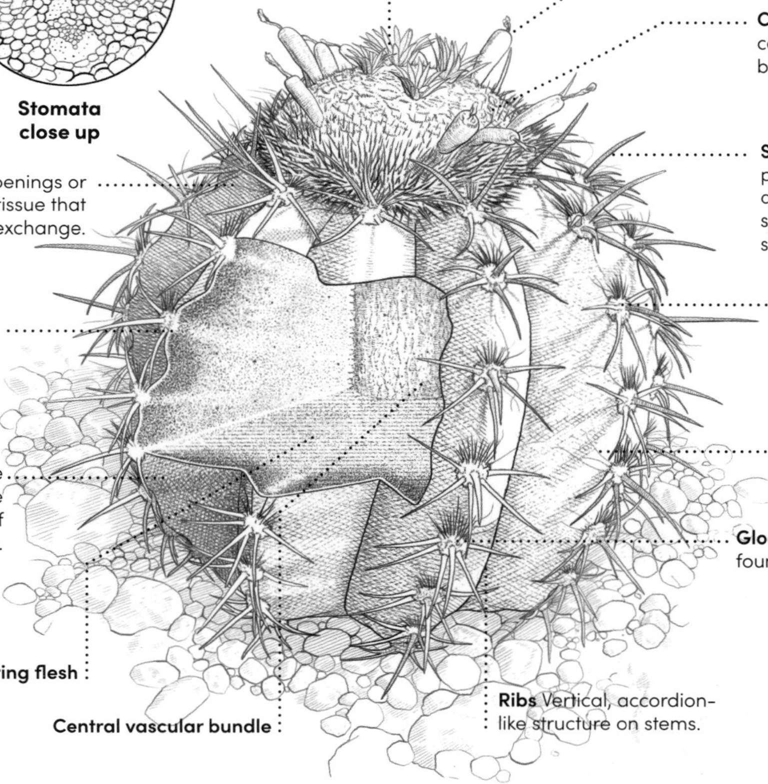

Flower The reproductive structure of the plant.
Fruit The fleshy or dry ripened ovary of a flowering plant, enclosing the seed or seeds.
Cephalium Fertile structure composed of densely packed, bristle-bearing areoles.
Stomata Tiny openings or pores in plant tissue that allow for gas exchange.
Spines A firm, slender, sharp-pointed structure, representing a modified leaf. A central spine grows from the areole, surrounded by radial spines.
Areole Equivalent to a bud, the areole is a round or elongated raised area from which spines, flowers, branches, or roots grow.
Tubercle A small, rounded projection on the stem. The areoles are located at the tips.
Trichomes Hair-like outgrowths from the areole.
Cuticle A protective waxy film covering the outermost skin layer of leaves and stems.
Glochids Tiny, barbed spines found in clusters on the areoles.
Water-storing flesh
Ribs Vertical, accordion-like structure on stems.
Central vascular bundle

Melocactus

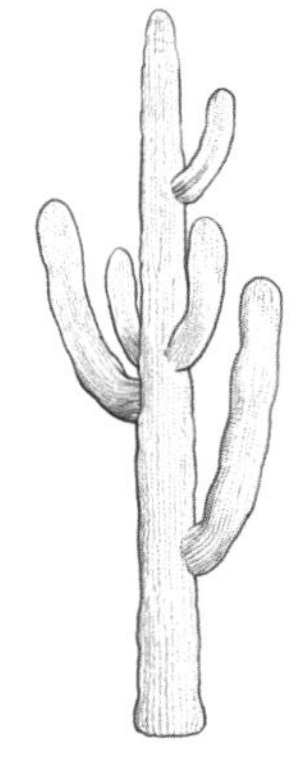

Arborescent cacti

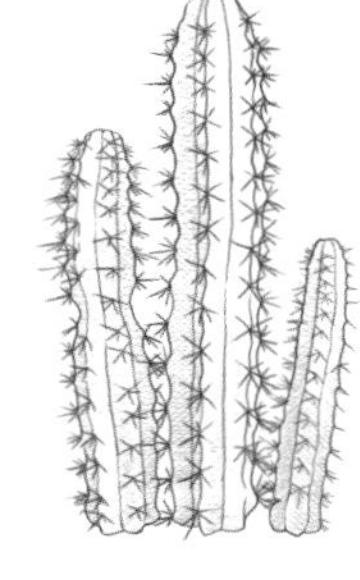

Columnar cacti

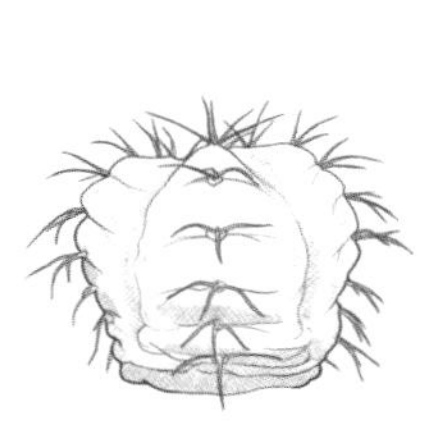

Globular cacti

Other forms

Growth habits

Cacti generally fall into four growth habits:

Arborescent cacti

Arborescent cacti generally resemble trees in terms of appearance. They are large, and have a woody trunk and many branches. Smaller, low-branching cacti are usually described as shrubby.

Columnar cacti

Columnar cacti mostly have vertical, cylinder-shaped stems, which may or may not branch. The main difference between arborescent and columnar is that there isn't a clear division into trunk and branches.

Globular cacti

Smaller-stemmed cacti can be described as globular (or globose). They generally have shorter, more ball-shaped stems than columnar cacti.

Other forms

Forest cacti have very different growth habits. Epiphytic and climbing cacti have flattened, leaf-like stems with few or even no spines. Some succulents can also be caudiciform plants. These feature a thickened, woody stem or root (caudex) that stores water for the plant to use in times of drought.

Fasciation

All plants rely on a growing point, known as the apical meristem or "growing tip". In most plants it is concentrated around a single point and produces cylindrical tissue, but a strange mutation in a single cell can change a plant's appearance so dramatically that it no longer resembles the original species. Fasciation, or cresting, is a rare phenomenon in plants, including cacti and other succulents. A mutation in the meristem cells can cause the growing point to become flattened and elongated, producing contorted tissue that results in some of the most weird and wonderful plants.

Although not fully understood, fasciation is thought to have various causes, including hormonal imbalances, random genetic mutation, infections, insect attack, exposure to cold and frost, or chemicals. Fasciation does not mean a plant is unhealthy. Commonly available examples are *Echeveria setosa* f. *cristata*, *Euphorbia lactea* 'Cristata', *Myrtillocactus geometrizans* f. *cristata* and *Mammillaria elongata* f. *cristata*, to name a few. Although they can look very different to the original species, care requirements for fasciated plants are the same as their normal counterparts.

Myrtillocactus geometrizans* f. *cristata

Flowers and fruit

Although cacti differ in appearance from other "normal" plants, their primary role in life is the same – to reproduce. There is something so beautifully incongruous about a cactus flower, which can be huge – bigger than the plant itself – and come in the most incredible intensity and variety of colours.

Some people don't realize that cacti can flower, which is often due to a misunderstanding of their care requirements or because the plant simply hasn't reached maturity. However, a cactus won't flower unless conditions are right. Once a cactus has reached maturity – and this can vary from species to species – it has the potential to flower, but even in its natural habitat, if conditions aren't ideal, it may decide to miss a year and try again the next, so don't be disheartened if yours hasn't yet.

Flowers

Flower buds emerge from modified structures called areoles (see page 14). Often, the youngest areoles at the tip of the stem produce flowers, but depending on the species, they can also grow from other points on the side of the stem.

Flowers of different species of cacti and succulents are programmed to open and close at different times of the day and night according to their habitat and the pollinators they want to attract. Some can self-seed by transferring their own pollen from stamen to stigma. Those that aren't self-fertile need help from moths, hummingbirds, bees, bats, and butterflies, which help to carry pollen from

Flowers of *Euphorbia resinifera* (top), *Echeveria secunda* var. *glauca* (middle), and *Disocactus × epiphyllum* (bottom).

flower to flower. In order to conserve energy and water, many cacti will open their flowers only when their preferred pollinators are active.

Amazingly, every year, as the cactus buds of saguaro and the organ pipe cactus (*Stenocereus thurberi*) begin to form, thousands of lesser long-nosed bats migrate north from their winter homes in central Mexico to feast on the nectar. When the bats emerge from the flowers, their heads are covered with pollen, which they take to the next flower they visit. After flowering, the cacti bear fruit, and the bats, along with other birds, ingest the seeds and poop them out, further spreading the potential for more plants to germinate.

Fruit and berries

Following fertilization, the flowers begin to wither and are replaced by fruit, berries, or pods containing seeds. The fruit's principal role is to aid in the spread of seeds, assuring the plant's reproductive success. Wind, water, and animals are essential factors in seed dispersal. Some seed pods, like those of *Lithops*, are programmed to open only when rained on so the seeds are washed out and have water with which to germinate.

The fruit of almost all cacti consists of a berry containing several or several hundreds of seeds. *Opuntia ficus-indica* produces a well-known fruit, the prickly pear, which is cultivated and consumed across the world (see page 138). Once peeled and the spines are removed, the flesh inside is soft, juicy, and reminiscent of melon in flavour.

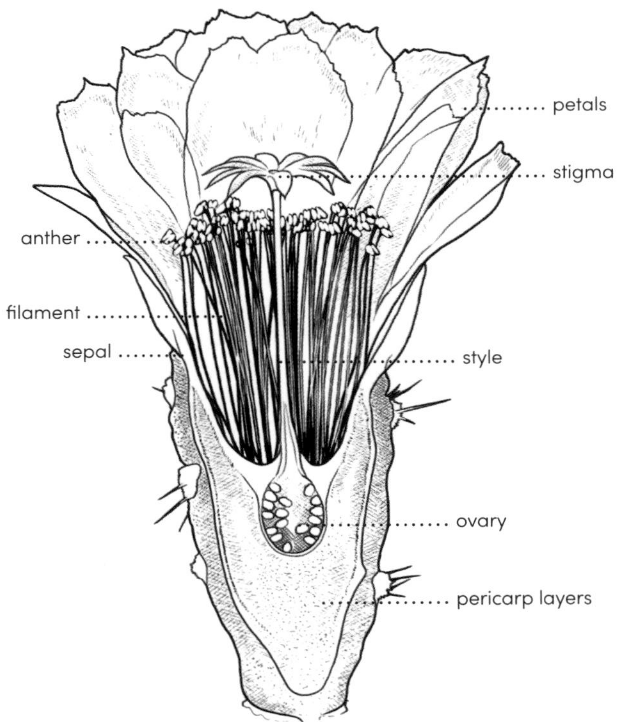

Flower reproductive system

Male parts comprise filaments and anthers, while the stigma, style, and ovary form the female parts. After pollination, the ovary bears the seed-containing fruit.

The fruit of *Myrtillocactus geometrizans* f. *cristata* (above left) and the unusual flowers of *Cleistocactus strausii* (above right).

History and uses

As varied and extensive as the plants themselves, the history and uses of cacti and other succulents spans continents and cultures, including everything from religious rituals and medicinal uses to construction materials and gastronomic delights.

Evidence suggests *Opuntia* was used in the human diet as early as 12,000 years ago, and it has been a staple in many cultures ever since. *Opuntia ficus-indica*, or prickly pear, has long been a crop plant, grown for its large, sweet fruits and the fleshy pads, known as "nopales", which taste like green beans and are used in salads and soups. Historically, *Opuntia* pulp has also been used to alleviate rashes, sunburn, haemorrhoids, and snake bites. Given its versatility, it is the most commercially important cactus in the world.

Psychoactive cactus *Lophophora williamsii* was historically used as an hallucinogen.

Spiritual uses

While many succulent plants have been cultivated for food, drink, and medicinal uses, others are ingested for spiritual rituals. Evidence exists of the use of mescaline, the psychoactive alkaloid found in peyote (*Lophophora williamsii*) and San Pedro cactus (*Trichocereus macrogonus* var. *pachanoi*) by native Americans for its hallucinogenic properties as long ago as 5,700 years. Archaeological samples have also identified the use of this powerful hallucinogen by the Peruvian Cupisnique people of 1500 BC and by many cultures since. To this day peyote is still used as a hallucinogen among some indigenous tribes of North and South America, where it holds great spiritual significance.

Cactus fruit are edible, but not all are as sweet and tasty as prickly pears.

Around AD 200–550, the Aztecs created a mildly psychotropic drink from *Agave*. The drink, known as "pulque", was used in religious rituals and is one of the oldest alcoholic fermented beverages in Mexico. Made from a handful of species of *Agave*, pulque could be considered the ancestral cousin of tequila. However, tequila can only be made from *Agave* 'Weber Azul'. Pulque has had a long history, during which it has been used as a "cure" for just about everything, from diabetes to sleep disorders. During the Aztec era, it was a sacred drink reserved for the gods and their priests. Today, this elixir has evolved into a recreational, beer-like libation.

A hunting tool

While cacti and other succulent plants have helped sustain human life, some other animals haven't been quite so lucky. Native to Baja California, Mexico, *Stenocereus gummosus* – long valued for its fruit – was once used as a tool for hunting. Fishing is a time-consuming activity with no guarantee of success unless, of course, the fish come to you. Fishers discovered that crushed *Stenocereus* stems released a toxic sap, which, when thrown into the water, stupefied the fish, allowing them to be scooped out. The poisonous sap of *Euphorbia* is also used for hunting. The Fali people of Northern Cameroon apply *Euphorbia kamerunica* sap to arrowheads to kill large animals such as antelopes.

Habitats in the wild

Say the word cactus to most people, and their minds will conjure up an image of a spiky plant living in a searingly hot desert, but cacti inhabit a wide diversity of climatic regions and ecosystems. While it is true that the majority of cacti and other succulents inhabit arid landscapes, approximately 10 per cent of species in the *Cactaceae* family live in humid forested regions of North, Central, and South America.

To make life simple, we can separate the cactus family into two different types: those that come from arid or semi-arid areas like deserts, rocky slopes, or sandy scrublands, which I refer to as arid habitat cacti (see page 104), and those that reside in forests (see page 148). Within these two distinct groups are species with different care requirements regarding light, substrate, and watering.

Rainfall, or the lack of it, is not the only thing that determines the habitats where succulent plants thrive. Another important factor is how long the period of drought lasts, as well as other climatic features, which determine what other vegetation can grow there.

Arid habitat cacti

Arid cacti live in arid and semi-arid regions, representing approximately one-third of the Earth's land surface. These areas, although diverse, are all characterized by drought, extreme temperature fluctuations, intense UV radiation, and poor soil. The term "desert" is too limiting for the habitat range where cacti grow, and you could be forgiven for thinking they only survive in warm areas. However, some species, such as those of the genus *Opuntia*, can survive frosts, snow, and extremely low

temperatures down to -30°C (-22°F). In harsh, arid environments of coastal cliffs, quarries, dunes, dry grasslands, deserts, prairies, and mountainous terrain, cacti reign supreme, conserving water to withstand drought and enduring great temperature extremes of searingly hot days and cold nights.

The common feature of these landscapes is the rocky, sandy soils, which retain little moisture, making them uninhabitable for most other non-succulent plants. Cacti are adept at absorbing rain quickly through a fibrous, spreading root system and storing it in their stems, which allows them to survive in some of the driest places on Earth, like areas of the Atacama Desert in Chile, where, despite some weather stations having never recorded ANY rainfall, cacti happily grow, surviving on the moisture from fog.

Forest habitat cacti

Forest cacti are epiphytic, anchoring themselves to trees, or lithophytic, clambering over rocks and branches, and gathering nutrients from decaying organic matter in crevices. Despite experiencing a lot of rain, the forests they inhabit are known as tropical dry forests because of the long dry season followed by months of heavy rainfall. These forest-dwellers belong to the subfamily *Cactoideae* and form two groups, *Hylocereae* and *Rhipsalideae*, the latter of which includes one of the most popular houseplants, *Schlumbergera*, or the Christmas cactus (see page 170).

Epiphytes cling to the branches and crevices of forest trees, and feed off decaying organic matter.

Where other succulent plants grow

While all cacti, apart from *Rhipsalis baccifera*, are native to the Americas, the distribution of other succulent plants is as diverse as their forms, with Africa playing host to around one-third of all species. Others are native to parts of Europe, Asia, Australia, the Americas, Madagascar, and the Canary Islands. With such wide distribution throughout the world, it would be foolish to attempt to describe every ecosystem, but it's important to mention one of the most significant: the Succulent Karoo. This area of the Karoo desert stretches along the Atlantic coast of Africa, from southwestern South Africa into southern Namibia and is home to one of the richest diversity of plants on Earth, with more than 6,000 species recorded; 40 per cent are endemic, meaning they're found nowhere else. Characterized by dunes, rocky hills, and desert plains, the landscape is one of extremes where temperatures range from -15°C (5°F) on the plateau in winter to over 40°C (104°F) on the plains in summer. Succulents such as *Lithops*, *Conophytum*, and *Agave* are found here.

Typical habitats

Desert

Receives an average rainfall of no more than 25cm (10in) and has little in the way

of vegetation. As the rain can be sporadic, cacti make use of heavy dews or coastal mists by absorbing moisture through spines or trichomes (see pages 14–15), which also serve as UV protection and help to insulate them from the cold.

Jungle
Has high humidity, with no significant differences between day- and nighttime temperatures. Cacti attach themselves to branches high up in the canopy or rocks where the trees filter light. Plants in the forest absorb nutrients from decaying leaves and other woodland detritus.

Mountainous terrain
While cacti are well adapted to hot, arid conditions, mountainous areas experience cooler temperatures, especially at higher altitudes, and the fluctuations between day and night can be significant. Most mountainous regions receive more rainfall than lowland deserts, resulting in a higher diversity of cacti species. The soil varies but is always free-draining and low in nutrients.

Grasslands
Temperate grasslands are open, grassy plains with rocky outcrops sparsely populated with trees. They can experience freezing temperatures, snow, and occasional wildfires. Low rainfall makes it an ideal environment for low-lying cacti, and spines are essential for protection against grazing animals. The soil is richer in nutrients than deserts or mountains.

Alpine zones
Winters can be severe with heavy snowfall, and summers are short. The temperature fluctuations between day and night are often significant. Plants grow in rocky crevices and gravelly soils, the rocky substrate providing stability and the gaps between the rocks offering protection from the wind.

Coastal areas
These regions typically experience moderate temperatures compared to inland areas, but can be prone to strong winds. Plants tend to be low-growing and clump-forming. Some plants supplement their water supply by capturing moisture from coastal fog and can tolerate, or even excrete, excess salt.

An aloe forest in full bloom, Karoo, South Africa.

Underground alliances

When we think of a typical desert, we might imagine a vast expanse of sand and little else. Compared to the rich, earthy, organic soil of a forest, teeming with organisms above and below ground, deserts appear to be little more than a carpet of lifeless sand. However, unseen to the naked eye, a remarkable ecosystem thrives on the surface of dryland soils, called the biocrust.

Studies estimate that biocrusts currently cover around 12 per cent of the Earth's land and approximately 30 per cent of all dryland soils, and yet their significance in supporting the growth of cacti and succulents is seldom acknowledged.

The biocrust

Soil biocrust is prevalent in places with little rainfall and, therefore, with fewer plants and more space between them, allowing sunlight to reach the soil surface. The crust-like structure, much like the crust of a loaf of bread, is often darker in colour and harder than what's underneath. Within this living "skin" are billions of microorganisms, including bacteria, fungi, algae, lichen, and mosses, which help prevent soil erosion, improve water retention, and contribute to nutrient cycling. A desert biocrust helps bind particles together, creating a more stable surface that isn't as vulnerable to the elements. Without the biocrust, germination would become more difficult, and there would be fewer plants, as this hardened surface protects seeds from being washed away or buried deep within the dry, sandy soil. The hardened crust also offers stability for the roots. Perhaps most fascinating is the beneficial relationship formed within the biocrust between xerophytic plants (adapted to survive in environments with limited water) and microorganisms. In this shallow, crusty layer live microfauna such as protozoa, nematodes, tardigrades,

The living biocrust in the Needles district of Canyonlands National Park, Utah.

rotifers, microarthropods, and mycorrhizal fungi. This ecosystem plays an essential role in cacti and succulent plant survival, contributing to nutrient availability by breaking down organic matter and fixing nitrogen, assisting the plant's nutrient uptake, which promotes healthy growth.

Don't bust the crust

Biocrusts vary in texture, microbial activity, and the presence of mosses, algae, lichen, and bacteria, depending on rainfall. In very dry regions, such as areas of the Atacama Desert, the biocrust has a smoother appearance because fewer organisms are present, while in wetter (but still arid) regions, it can be much rougher, resembling the burnt topping of an apple crumble. This "topping", however, is fragile and can easily be damaged by humans walking over it. In Moab, Utah, in the US, tourists are reminded, "Don't bust the crust," because it can take hundreds of years to recover. Awareness of the importance of the biocrust – not only for plants but for humans too – is growing. Biocrusts protect the Earth from erosion and play a valuable role in the diversity and productiveness of xeric soils that sustain plants, wildlife, and agriculture.

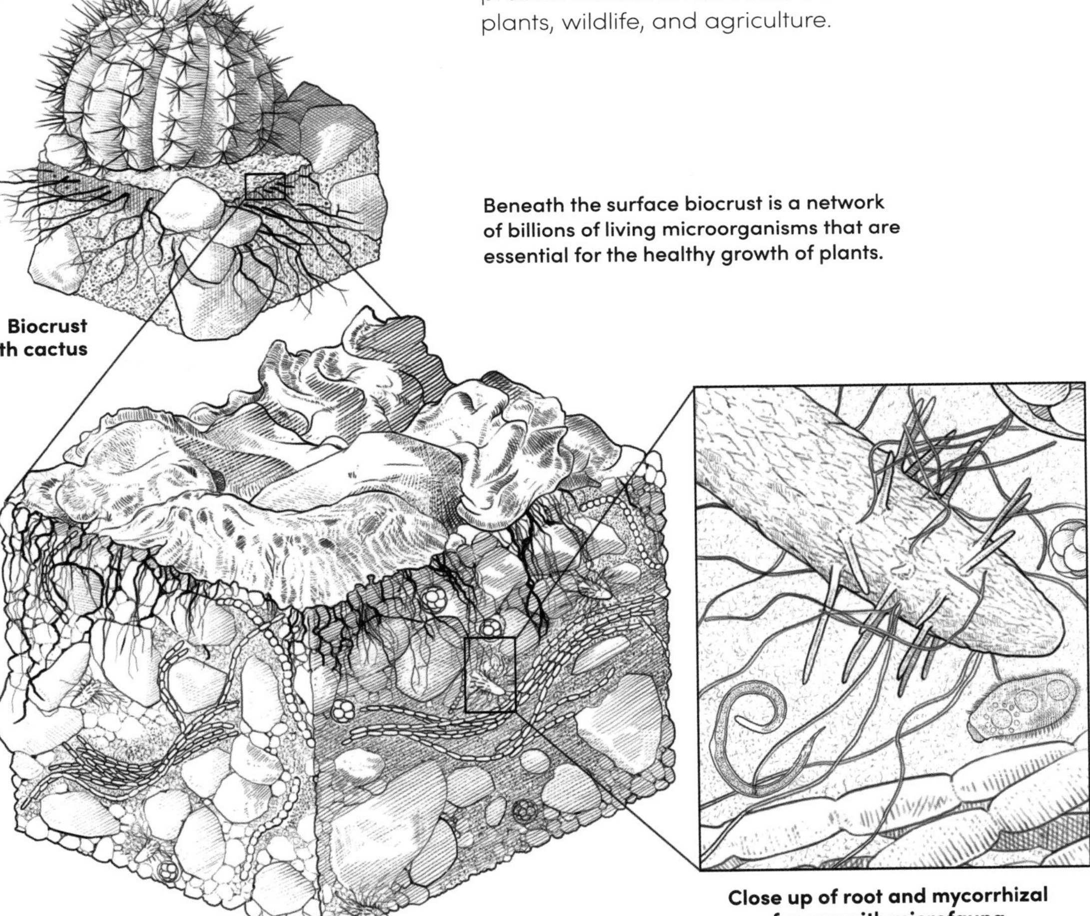

Beneath the surface biocrust is a network of billions of living microorganisms that are essential for the healthy growth of plants.

Biocrust with cactus

Close up of root and mycorrhizal fungus with microfauna

Close up section of biocrust

Where the wild cacti grow

Once bitten by the succulent plant bug, if time and money allow, there can be no better way to appreciate these remarkable plants than to see them in their natural habitat.

Most continents in the world have arid areas, and various plants have adapted to cope with these challenging environments, but the plants most interesting to cacti and succulent enthusiasts are those living in the dry regions of Africa and the Americas. Although Mexico, Bolivia, Argentina, and Peru have the highest concentration of cacti, the easiest and least intrusive places to see them are in designated national parks in the United States.

National parks

Arizona has many breathtaking parks where you can see the iconic, monolithic saguaro (*Carnegiea gigantea*). Top of the list is Saguaro National Park near Tucson. Here, you can walk through the park's trails and get up close to these majestic giants. On the border with the Mexican State of Sonora is the Organ Pipe Cactus National Monument, a UNESCO biosphere reserve and the only place in the United States where the huge *Stenocereus thurberi* (organ pipe cactus) grows wild.

From Arizona across the border into California is Joshua Tree National Park. This unique park straddles the Colorado Desert and Mojave Desert and is home to the magnificent *Yucca brevifolia*, aka the Joshua tree, which isn't a tree but a succulent plant that resembles a tree.

In Mexico, the Chihuahuan Desert, the Sonoran Desert, and the Tehuacán Valley are the richest areas of cactus diversity, where a great number of globular cacti and *Opuntioideae* species are found. Succulents such as *Yucca faxoniana* (commonly

The statuesque *Yucca brevifolia* lends its common name to the Joshua Tree National Park, California (above). Organ Pipe Cactus National Monument, in the Sonoran Desert, is the only place in the US where *Stenocereus thurberi* grows (opposite).

known as giant daggers) and *Agave victoriae-reginae* (see page 185) are also common.

The Tehuacán-Cuicatlán valley is separated from the Chihuahua Desert by the Trans-Mexican volcanic mountain belt. This region has the highest concentrations of columnar cacti in the world, including the massive *Cephalocereus tetetzo*.

The Sonoran Desert covers the northwestern Mexican states of Sonora, Baja California, Baja California Sur, and part of the southwestern United States. It is one of the hottest deserts on Earth. Notable Sonoran desert species are *Stenocereus thurberi* (organ pipe cactus), *Carnegiea gigantea* (saguaro), and various *Opuntia* species.

The mountains of northwestern Argentina and Bolivia are hotspots for cacti diversity. At higher altitudes are species such as *Gymnocalycium bruchii*, and lower down the mountains, *Stetsonia coryne* (toothpick cactus) grow.

The Atacama Desert in Chile is considered one of the driest coastal deserts and the largest fog desert in the world. This protected area has a vast array of cacti and succulents, including the striking *Copiapoa cinerea* and *Copiapoa columna-alba*.

When visiting any plants in their natural habitat, take photos as a souvenir, but never cuttings or pieces of plant that have fallen on the ground. Many cacti and succulent plants are critically endangered because of habitat loss and poaching.

The cactus and succulent garden at the Huntington Botanical Gardens, California.

The arid zone in the Princess of Wales Conservatory at Royal Botanic Gardens, Kew.

Botanical gardens

While seeing plants in habitat is remarkable, it's not always possible, so visiting botanical gardens is an excellent alternative.

The Huntington Botanical Gardens, San Marino, California

This desert garden has one of the world's biggest and oldest collections of cacti and other succulents in the world. More than a century old, it showcases over 2,000 different species. There are some astonishing specimens of *Agave*, an impressive display of the golden barrel cactus (*Echinocactus grusonii*), and spectacular *Beaucarnea recurvata*.

Royal Botanic Gardens, Kew, London

Kew Gardens was founded in 1759 and is listed as a UNESCO World Heritage Site because it houses the largest and most diverse botanical and mycological collections in the world. In 1987 the Princess of Wales Conservatory opened; a glasshouse of zoned ecosystems, including arid and tropical areas home to an impressive array of terrestrial and epiphytic cacti and other succulent plants.

Sukkulenten-Sammlung, Zürich

The Zurich Succulent Plant Collection has been home to one of the largest and most important specialist collections of succulent plants since 1931. Experience 6,500 different species from 80 plant families in the greenhouses. Outside in the cold frames are low-growing cacti and a rockery with winter-hardy cacti and other succulents.

The Desert Botanical Garden in Phoenix, Arizona (opposite).

Kirstenbosch National Botanical Gardens, South Africa

On the eastern slopes of Cape Town's Table Mountain, Kirstenbosch is one of the world's most biodiverse gardens and a leader in conservation science. The gardens are a UNESCO World Heritage Site showcasing over 7,000 species, many of them rare, indigenous, and endangered. The conservatory contains some interesting species from the Namib Desert including *Welwitschia mirabilis*, believed to be a relic of the Jurassic period.

Desert Botanical Garden, Arizona

This garden offers one of the world's finest collections of xeric plants in an incredible outdoor setting. It has more than 50,000 desert plants, which can be accessed on five thematic trails. If you are unable to walk far or are tight for time, the Desert Botanical Gardens are the next best thing to seeing cacti and other desert plants in their natural habitat. Be sure to visit the wildflower trail and the first cactus to be planted in the garden in 1939, a *Stenocereus eruca*, which can still be seen crawling along the ground.

Botanical Garden Munich-Nymphenburg

Opened in 1812, the gardens have an awe-inspiring complex of glasshouses. The tour begins in the first of the big halls, the large cactus house, home to mighty agaves, columnar cacti, and golden barrel cacti. Travel on through the extensive greenhouses and enter another large hall where the Africa and Madagascar plant collection is housed.

The poaching issue

We think of cacti and succulents as hardy, surviving in harsh habitats with very little water. But many species are exceptionally vulnerable, with almost a third of known cacti in danger of extinction from illegal poaching, and other succulent plants such as *Lithops* so critically endangered that some species may soon become extinct.

Cacti and other succulents are among the most sought-after plants in the world. Their striking characteristics have for centuries allured plant enthusiasts and collectors, many of whom believe themselves to be conservationists, rather than contributing to the peril of many species. While the majority of the cacti and succulent trade is sustained by artificial propagation, demand for wild specimens continues to pose a threat, particularly to species endemic to only one region, desert, or hillside. In 2020 "Operation Atacama", an undercover operation investigating the criminal networks behind illicit cacti trading, seized more than 1,000 of some of the world's rarest cacti, valued at over $1.2 million on the black market. The operation highlighted not only the volume of plants being stripped from the wild, but just how much money traffickers may be earning from the trade.

Endangered plants

While most people are aware of animal poaching, far fewer give thought to the plants on the brink of extinction. "The basic functioning of the planet would effectively grind to a halt without plants, but people care more about animals," said Jared Margulies, author of *The Cactus Hunters*. In 2023 approximately 25 per cent of mammals were classed as endangered, while over 30 per cent of the world's approximate 1,800 cactus species were recorded as threatened with extinction.

In the Saguaro National Park in Arizona, while the visitors look up to admire the sheer size and beauty of saguaro cacti, the rangers are busy looking down for holes in the ground. Saguaros grow only 2.5–4cm (1–1½in) in the first eight years of their life, and can take 50–100 years to grow "arms". Unfortunately this makes mature specimens a target for poachers who command a high price for large examples. Officials have had to resort to microchipping them in a bid to stop thieves, which so far has proven to be a successful deterrent.

Stripping plants from the wild has far-reaching environmental implications. Their absence from the landscape removes a source of food for pollinators, shelter for various organisms, and protection from predators. The disturbed soil allows for opportunistic non-native plant species to get a foothold and increases soil erosion, leading to landslides.

Stopping the illegal trading of plants is critical for the survival of those species at risk, but also helps those who are acting responsibly and trading plants within the law. Discouraging illegal online selling gives genuine traders and plant lovers a platform where they can shop with confidence.

Prized saguaro cacti in Arizona have to be microchipped to deter thieves.

How to Grow

Growing basics

Generalizing on the topic of plant care is particularly difficult. People grow plants in different environments, indoors or outside, in different climate zones across the world. Guidance can vary from country to country, state to state, garden to garden, and therefore may not apply to your particular growing conditions. However, there are some specific rules and essential care advice that apply to all cacti and other succulent plants.

The essentials

There are four main steps to get right in order for a plant to survive and thrive: light (see page 38), substrate (see page 44), water (see page 48), and temperature (see page 52) – plus an extra one for bonus points: the pH level of the substrate (see page 56).

How much light a plant needs depends on its type and where it originates. How to water it depends on how much light it receives, the substrate it is grown in, the air temperature and humidity, and whether the plant is indoors, in a greenhouse, or outside. All these factors play a part in its care needs, which is why some rules are hard to define.

Key to the success of growing any plant is a basic understanding of their natural habitat. You can plop a cactus on a windowsill and it will probably survive, but for it to reach its full potential, you need to put in some groundwork.

Match the light your plant receives in its natural environment and you will have a good chance of it surviving. Get the substrate, water, and temperature right, and these factors combined will create the ideal conditions for your plant to photosynthesize and grow.

Right plant, right place

Our challenge as growers is to replicate a plant's natural habitat as best we can within the conditions dictated by our location in the world. Here in the UK, we are famous for having grey skies and lots of rain, coupled with subzero temperatures in winter – the perfect recipe for creating cactus mush. Having said that, it isn't impossible to grow cacti and succulent plants outside in the UK (as you'll see on page 88), as long as you choose plants that can tolerate cold, damp weather conditions. Growing in a greenhouse mitigates the problem of rain and, if heated, the cold too. But if you don't have the luxury of outside space or a greenhouse, you can successfully raise happy, healthy cacti and other succulent plants indoors if you position them in the right place, where you can prioritize their growing needs.

Cacti and succulents are among the most undemanding plants to share a home with, due to their ability to withstand long periods of drought, but to do this, they need to be given the right conditions.

Recreating the natural environment of cacti and succulents as best you can is key to their growing success.

Light

The most important factor in caring for cacti and other succulent plants is undoubtedly light. Healthy growth for all plants relies upon adequate sunlight for photosynthesis. There are few – if any – that can grow properly in a permanently shady spot. In these conditions, most will etiolate, growing weak and their stems thinning, or drop all their leaves, before dying a slow, hungry death.

Humans can survive for a limited period without food. It's no different for light-starved plants, be it for a few months or maybe years. Ultimately, however, there is no happy ending for a plant denied access to enough light to photosynthesize. It won't ever thrive and is more likely to develop ailments and become susceptible to pests. There is little point in buying a cactus or succulent if you then position it without considering its most basic light-intensity needs.

I have to stop myself from shouting at the TV when I watch interior designers on room-makeover programmes putting cacti on a bookshelf at the opposite end of the room to the window, or succulents on a desk nowhere near sunlight. These plants may look nice temporarily, but unless there is a grow light above them (see page 40), they will not survive long term. No one buys a plant to experience the joy of watching it die, so give it the best chance of a long life and healthy growth by providing the light it needs.

A position near a window is best for cacti and succulents, to maximize light availability.

Growing under glass can offer cacti and succulents all the light they need, and the protection allows for a diverse collection.

Natural light

Our homes, even those with large glass sliding doors or skylights, are by their very nature darker than a greenhouse or the outside world, owing to the simple fact that they have a roof. Nonetheless, although it can pose challenges, you can still grow a thriving collection of plants indoors. I live in a 1930s semi-detached suburban house in the Southeast of England, which is about as far removed as you can get from the natural habitat of xerophytes, and yet despite this, each year, I have many cacti and succulents flowering indoors.

A common misconception is that all cacti and succulents like full sun, when in truth many often grow beneath other plants in semi-shade, which makes them ideal houseplants. However, it is worth remembering that semi-shade outside is much brighter than semi-shade indoors. All cacti (except those from forests; see page 148) need to be on the brightest windowsill or in a conservatory or greenhouse (see overleaf) to thrive, whereas some other succulent plants can tolerate slightly lower light conditions, notably *Dracaena trifasciata* (see page 202), which adapts easily to a more shaded area of a room. This does not mean, however, that you should put it in a shady spot when it would invariably prefer at least a few hours of direct sunlight a day, close to a bright window. Just because a plant can tolerate less light doesn't mean it should when it doesn't have to.

Artificial light

Placing cacti on a windowsill or in a conservatory where they can receive direct sunlight all day is ideal. However, in dark homes, cloudy regions, or during the winter months, natural light might not be sufficient, and you might want to consider using supplementary lighting.

Full-spectrum grow lights replicate sunlight and can be used when natural sunlight is inadequate, i.e. during winter. A standard light bulb brightens a dark room but doesn't provide the different wavelengths needed for plants to grow. Full-spectrum grow lights, on the other hand, offer a much richer light spectrum, emphasizing red, blue, and green light, and all the colours inbetween, for optimal plant growth. Find out more about growing cacti and other succulents with grow lights on page 42.

Growing under glass

Those ready to take their xerophyte obsession to the next level might want to consider a greenhouse, which provides the opportunity to grow a far wider variety of cacti and succulents, including large columnar ones that wouldn't fit on a windowsill. Greenhouses provide far greater light intensity than indoors, so much so that it can be necessary to shade the glass in extremely hot and sunny weather to prevent plants scorching.

I grow cacti and succulents both inside our house and in a greenhouse, and the difference in the speed of growth and willingness to flower is noticeable, which is no surprise when considering the upgrade in light intensity from inside to outside. It wasn't until having a greenhouse that I properly noticed spines. I know that sounds ridiculous, as cacti are covered in them, but I don't think I appreciated before how much light affects the appearance of their spines in colour, size, and abundance. After spending 20 years inside its previous owner's home, my *Cleistocactus strausii* became beautifully white and yeti-like in my greenhouse. The soft, long spines now completely obscure the stems, which they hadn't done before, helping to protect the plant from cold and excessive heat – a necessity in their native habitat.

A greenhouse is the perfect solution for those who live in seasonally cold, wet climates, as it allows maximum sunlight

When natural light levels are not intense enough indoors, consider using grow lights to replicate the spectrum of sunlight.

without rain. During the warmer months, though, care needs to be taken to provide adequate ventilation and sometimes shading. Glass provides a surface for condensation to gather, raising the humidity, and acts as a magnifying glass, which can burn plants. The temperature inside a greenhouse can far exceed that of the outside, which can also inhibit growth or even damage the plant, so opening vents, windows, and doors is essential for air circulation.

Greenhouses can be ideal for growing in cold, wet climates with lower light levels, but still, plants may need shading in intense sun.

While there are a few downsides to growing under glass, these are far outweighed by the benefits. Fully understanding and appreciating the importance of light intensity can only really be achieved by seeing plants growing in a greenhouse or, better still, outside, as nature intended.

Grower profile

Luke Ricketts

Location Paignton, Devon

Specialism Growing under artificial lighting

Membership British Cactus and Succulent Society

Luke is a passionate indoor grower with unique expertise in growing cacti and succulents under artificial light. Through trial and error, he has gained a wealth of knowledge about how to cultivate a healthy collection indoors.

Luke with his Shiba Inu dog, Yoshi, alongside a crop of indoor *Trichocereus pachanoi* seedlings, thriving under grow lights.

How long have you been growing?

I've always been around green-fingered people, although it didn't start for me until 2020. I was playing a videogame that allowed you to breed flowers. I mentioned this in passing to my father, who suggested I try a real plant. He said his Christmas cactus (*Schlumbergera truncata*) was very low maintenance. I bought one of my own and things spiralled from there!

What are the main challenges of growing under artificial light?

1. **Light demands.** There's no rule book on how you should set up your lighting. It is recommended to use an illuminometer to work out the distance from your plants and the lighting schedule. It's also worth considering the natural habitat of the plants.

2. **Humidity.** This can be a serious killer for cacti grown indoors because stagnant air has nowhere to go. I have a range of fans in use all the time to move the air around, because generally desert plants are exposed to a lot of wind.

3. **Energy demands.** LED light boards are the most energy-efficient method, but there is no getting away from the costs involved.

4. **Space.** You're usually restricted to where the lighting can actually reach in a grow tent or on shelving. There will never be enough room, and I've had to upgrade my set-up many times to accommodate more plants.

What advice would you give beginners looking to replicate your set-up?

I would try getting a propagator with lights first and sowing your own seeds. This takes up much less space and is the least costly method. Depending on how slow-growing the species is, this will give you a year or so to research what will work for you and to

A top shelf packed with various grafted specimens, *Euphorbia abdelkuri*, and a *Copiapoa cinerea*, and beneath, many *Lophophora williamsii* cultivars.

get everything set up so the seedlings can be moved out of the tank. I'd also look for shelving that is confirmed to take heavy weights, and recommend buying from a reputable lighting brand.

Five plants everyone should grow?

The five I've chosen all have significant issues with poaching from the wild. I think as growers we should be responsible for getting as much plant material out there to drive prices of "collectable" species down to lessen the strain on populations found in nature.

1. ***Lophophora.*** This spineless cactus has a reputation as a difficult plant, but I've never had that experience with them. They grow in many substrates and flower many times in a season if they feel like it.

2. ***Dioscorea elephantipes.*** These caudiciforms are a lesson in slow growing, but they keep getting more beautiful as they age, and no two mature plants ever look the same.

3. ***Astrophytum.*** There are so many wonderful cultivars of this plant, it's almost unbelievable that the genus only has six species! Growers from Asia, in particular, have really pushed the boundaries of what is possible with selective breeding.

4. ***Ariocarpus.*** In nature, these plants are masters of crypsis (camouflage) and blend into their rocky environments extremely well.

5. ***Pseudolithos cubiformis.*** These are very difficult to buy and even more difficult to keep alive. Their flowers produce the smell of rotting carrion to flies, which act as pollinators. Very niche, but great to look at.

What are your top tips for plant care?

Don't be afraid to make mistakes and experiment. Cacti and succulents are born to survive in some of the harshest conditions. Remember that less is more; it's much harder to kill these plants from underwatering than overwatering. Join the online community; there are lots of friendly people out there who are willing to impart decades of knowledge given the chance. And most importantly, have fun!

Substrates

Cacti and other succulents need a healthy root system to thrive, so choosing the right substrate is key. While water is an essential element for the survival of all plants, it can also contribute to their demise.

Roots need oxygen, so the substrate must be aerobic, allowing free air movement. Anaerobic soil is caused by the air pockets being filled by water, which starves the roots of oxygen and becomes a breeding ground for bacteria, leading to root rot. A substrate made up of large as well as smaller particles will allow water to travel through it quickly, so oxygen can circulate around the roots.

Start by determining where your plant comes from in the wild, as this will provide the best guide to the substrate it prefers. If it comes from a rocky outcrop, replicate this with a rocky potting mix. If its natural habitat is the branch of a tree, make sure the substrate contains a high percentage of chunky bark to help it feel at home.

The growing medium for most cacti and succulents should drain quickly, mimicking their natural environment. Below is a list of components that can be used. They are classified as either organic or inorganic; combining the two helps provide nutrients for the plant, while also creating generous air pockets for oxygen to circulate.

Almost all substrates you might want to use have an environmental impact. Many products, although natural, might not have been extracted in an environmentally sensitive way or might have travelled many miles to reach your home. Try to choose the least damaging materials where possible, though of course this will vary depending on your geographical location and the source of the product.

Potting compost (organic)

This is usually made from materials such as coconut coir, composted bark, green waste, grit, and sand. The organic matter helps to retain moisture and supplies the plant with a range of nutrients. Cacti and succulents from arid habitats aren't used to moisture-retentive soil, so adding other components into potting compost to make it free-draining is very important. Make sure the compost is peat-free before buying.

Potting compost

Horticultural charcoal (organic)

Also known as biochar or activated charcoal, this is a charcoal-like substance made by burning organic material from agricultural and forestry wastes in a controlled process called pyrolysis (heating in the absence of oxygen). The result is a highly porous, stable form of carbon with a neutral pH that can improve soil structure, allowing for better aeration and drainage, and also help provide a habitat for beneficial microorganisms and mycorrhizal fungi. It can help to absorb water and retain nutrients, making them available to plants over and extended period of time.

Horticultural charcoal

Bark (organic)

A versatile component, particularly beneficial for epiphytic cacti and succulents that naturally grow on trees. Not the same as bark sold as an outdoor mulch, this bark (sold as a substrate for orchids) is typically made from fir or pine trees and provides excellent aeration and drainage, mimicking the loose, airy substrate that plants living on trees are used to. It is a by-product of the timber trade, which is then processed and steamed so it's more resistant to mould and rot. Check that the bark you buy is from forestry-certified sources.

Bark

Perlite (inorganic)

Perlite is perhaps the best-known and most commonly used additive in horticulture. Made from naturally occurring volcanic glass, it expands when heated, like popping corn, generating tiny, lightweight particles that resemble Styrofoam. Perlite is chemically inert and sterile, making it ideal for hydroponic growing. It can also be used to propagate seeds and cuttings but is chiefly used for improving soil structure and aiding airflow. In pots, it helps slow down soil compaction, allowing water to quickly pass through the potting mix.

Perlite

Pumice (inorganic)

A light-coloured, porous igneous rock formed during volcanic eruptions. As it is lightweight, pumice makes an excellent addition to a potting mix to increase drainage and airflow and prevent the soil from compacting. It has a neutral pH, doesn't retain moisture, and can also be used as a decorative form of topdressing.

Pumice

Horticultural grit (inorganic)

Grit is usually made from coarse sand or small, broken rock, and has long been favoured in gardening and landscaping. It comes in a variety of particle sizes, and is usually made from crushed granite, limestone, or quartz. Adding grit to a potting mix decreases soil compaction, promotes drainage, and improves aeration. It can also be applied as a topdressing to help prevent erosion, especially in container gardens or locations prone to frequent or heavy rainfall, and helps give weight to a pot so it doesn't fall over. It's often used in alpine and rock gardens, where well-drained soils are essential. One of the cheaper options and readily available to buy.

Horticultural grit

Zeolite (inorganic)

Zeolite is a naturally occurring mineral, formed from the interaction of volcanic ash with alkaline groundwater. It has a unique porous structure that allows for high cation exchange – in simple terms, it attracts and holds on to positively charged ions like calcium, magnesium, and potassium, which is important for enhancing the fertility of the soil without the risk of overfertilization. Its ability to trap and slowly release water makes it ideal for plants that require a balance of moisture and air in the root zone.

Zeolite

Sand (inorganic)

One of the most common components used in cacti and succulent mixes. Its primary role is to improve soil drainage and prevent waterlogging. Opt for coarse sand rather than fine play sand, as the latter can lead to compacted soil – the opposite of the desired effect. A large particle size ensures that water drains quickly and air pockets are maintained. Sand is a widely available resource, but sourcing it responsibly is essential.

Sand

Akadama (inorganic)

Akadama is a naturally occurring, granulated clay, predominantly used in bonsai cultivation. Sourced from Japan, this clay has a unique ability to retain water and nutrients, which are gradually released as the plant requires. This helps mimic the natural growing conditions of many cacti and succulents, which often experience intermittent rainfall. Akadama porosity helps promote excellent aeration, essential for healthy root growth. It also darkens in colour when moist, which can help determine when to water. The downsides are that in cold, wet climates the granules are said to progressively break down into smaller particles that can inhibit, rather than increase, drainage.

Akadama

Cat litter (inorganic)

No, your eyes aren't deceiving you – certain types of cat litter can be a very effective soil amendment, similar to akadama but without the price tag. The key is to choose a non-clumping, unscented litter made from 100 per cent fired clay granules, also called moler clay. This type of litter has excellent water-absorption properties, retaining it when necessary and draining the excess. It also provides good aeration. Check the product specifications thoroughly, or you could cause serious damage to your plants – in the UK only one or two brands are suitable.

Cat litter

Watering

Xerophytes have unique water requirements, which replicate their original conditions as closely as possible. They have a grab-it-and-grow attitude to moisture collection and would therefore be confused by having water constantly available, so the number-one killer of succulent plants is soggy, dense, anaerobic soil. When water remains in the soil for a prolonged period, it fills up the air pockets, blocking oxygen from the roots, leading to a build-up of bacteria that causes them to rot.

In nature, succulent plants obtain water in two ways: from heavy dews, when droplets collect on the stem, spines, or trichomes and are absorbed or trickle down to the roots, or from rainfall. Drought-tolerant plants either develop deep tap roots to access the groundwater or shallow roots, eagerly awaiting unpredictable rainfalls. Opuntias and agaves can also develop "rain roots" in response to moisture, which emerge from lateral root buds within a few hours of the soil being wet and dry out when the rainwater disappears. Some plants in shallow soils can even grow their roots upwards to collect water quickly, while others, such as aloes, have developed funnel-like rosettes of succulent leaves, which collect dew and direct it downwards, where the plant can utilize it.

The key is to create a balance by using the correct substrate (see page 44), where water is retained briefly and then allowed to drain away. The frequency of watering depends on several factors, including sunlight, temperature, humidity, the size of the pot, and even the porosity of what the pot is made from, which all in some way influence soil moisture.

Always test moisture levels in the substrate before watering by pushing your finger into the pot.

The golden rule

Before watering, it's essential to check the substrate by pushing your finger into the pot or weighing it in your hands to gauge the soil moisture level. When the pot feels light, or your finger remains clean when you pull it out of the substrate, saturate evenly around the plant until water starts to run out of the drainage holes. This method makes sure that the entire root system, not just the surface, gets moisture. After watering, always allow the soil to fully drain before putting the plant into a decorative cover.

Watering in dormancy

Winter in the northern hemisphere, particularly at higher latitudes, can be dark, and the days short, reducing light intensity and affecting photosynthesis. This may trigger a period of dormancy when growth slows down significantly and, as a result, the water requirements of our plants decrease. During this period, overwatering becomes a much greater risk than underwatering.

If you live in a country that gets cold and dark during winter, you can expect most cacti to enter dormancy from late October to April, and they should, on the whole, be kept dry during this period. Instead of stopping abruptly, however, water less frequently in the weeks leading up to the resting period. Forest cacti will still require water throughout the winter months, but less often than in the warmer months. Other succulent plants might need watering once a month or less depending on their

Adjust your watering with the seasons, whether growing indoors, outdoors, or under glass.

growth cycle – *Lithops* (see page 224) and *Conophytum* (see page 192) are exceptions. Observe any changes, such as shrivelling, which can mean the plant needs water, but always check the substrate first to ensure it is completely dry before watering. Always remember, if in doubt, don't water!

To catch any water that might roll off the surface or drain out, try watering in a tray.

Watering during active growth

Cacti and succulents originate from different climates (temperate, tropical, desert) but are similar in that each environment has periodic or prolonged drought. Throughout the year, due to seasonal changes and, importantly, their growth cycle, their water requirements will vary. In spring and summer, encouraged by increased daylight hours and warmer temperatures, most cacti enter their active growth phase, which in turn increases their water requirements. During this period, the soil should dry out completely between waterings. Depending on light intensity and temperature, this could mean watering once a week or every other week, depending on the specific conditions inside your home or outside in a greenhouse or garden.

You might find that the substrate has become so dry it is hydrophobic, such that instead of water being absorbed, it rolls off the surface. In this instance, it might be necessary to sit the pot in a tray filled with water or to fully submerge it for 5–10 minutes to ensure the substrate is properly saturated.

If the substrate is so dry that it has become hydrophobic, sit the pot in a water bath.

When to water

It's best to water plants in the morning, allowing them to dry out during the day when temperatures are warmer and they are better equipped to absorb moisture efficiently. During the evening, temperatures tend to drop, which can lead to water sitting in the soil for longer periods without evaporating. Cold soil combined with moisture, particularly in regions with cooler nights, can lead to issues such as rot or fungal disease (see page 90).

Types of water

There are various types of water that can be used, each with pros and cons. Understanding their individual properties and potential effects on your plants will allow you to make the best decision for their health.

Rainwater

This is the best option for plants, but it is not always readily available. It lacks the added chemicals and heavy mineral content of tap water and mimics the natural watering conditions in native habitats. A water butt is the best way to collect rainwater, but buckets will do. If you don't have access to a garden, you can collect rainwater in containers secured to a window ledge.

Reverse osmosis (RO) water

This is another excellent option for watering cacti – systems can be fitted to your mains water supply or purchased at aquatic shops. The filtering process removes impurities, including chlorine, fluoride, and dissolved minerals. The result is highly purified water, free from additives. However, because it's so pure, it does lack essential minerals, and you may need to add fertilizer to ensure the plants remain healthy.

Tap water

The easiest and most accessible type of water, but as it contains various chemicals, such as chlorine and fluoride, and dissolved minerals like calcium and magnesium, it can, over time, lead to a build-up in the soil, which can have a detrimental effect on roots. It's therefore advisable to occasionally flush the soil with rainwater.

Softened tap water

Some areas have hard water, formed when it passes through limestone or chalk, which contains a high level of minerals. Water softeners can be installed in homes, which usually replace calcium with sodium. However, it's not advisable to rely on softened water for your plants, as overuse will cause a build-up of salt in the soil.

Inline tap filter water

Water from inline tap filters is a compromise between tap water and the purity of RO water. These filters can significantly reduce the heavy metals and other contaminants in tap water.

Water collected from a dehumidifier

If you use a dehumidifier, don't throw out the water. Make use of it to water your cacti and succulents.

Water until saturated and then allow any excess water to drain away fully.

Temperature

Temperature is one of the main environmental factors that affect the growth of plants; it's also one of the defining reasons why certain species only grow in certain places in the world. The native habitats of different cacti and succulents often dictate their tolerance ranges, which is important to bear in mind when growing them at home. While it is true that these plants inhabit warm climates, many have adapted to withstand a significant seasonal drop in temperature.

In general, plants grow when it's warm and are dormant when it's cold, but even cacti and succulents have their limits and can stop growing in extreme heat or die in extreme cold. Xerophytic plants inhabit a broad range of climates, from extreme deserts to the wet tropics, but despite this diversity, the optimum daytime temperature range for many species falls on average between 20°C and 30°C (68°F and 86°F). In warm weather, indoor plants will enjoy being moved outside, but take care not to put them into intense direct sunlight until they have had time to adapt, as this can cause them to permanently scorch.

Growing outdoors can be successful in a range of climates, if the specific conditions are taken into account.

Impact on watering

Higher temperatures increase the evaporation rate, drying out the substrate faster, which is why most plants require more frequent watering during the warmer months. CAM plants (see page 13), which perform a special type of photosynthesis to conserve water, open their stomata at night for gas exchange instead of during the heat of the day. However, during a heatwave, stomata may close during the day and night to minimize water loss, affecting the plant's ability to capture CO_2, and this can slow growth. Tissue damage

Cacti and succulents can thrive in a warm home with the right watering. Some forest-dwellers will even enjoy the humidity of a bathroom.

can also occur at extremely high temperatures, so it's strongly advisable to shade plants growing outside, particularly in a greenhouse.

While extreme heat is dangerous, cacti and succulents are at far greater risk of dying at the opposite end of the temperature spectrum. Cold, combined with water, is a killer. As light and temperature levels drop, many plants enter a period of dormancy and require little to no water. Some cacti and succulents don't like being colder than 10°C (50°F), while others can tolerate lower, but only if kept dry. When the temperature falls below this, indoors or out, it's best to stop watering, while greenhouses should be insulated and heated or the plants brought inside.

Awareness of how temperature can impact plants and adjusting our care accordingly is essential. In a centrally heated home, the average room temperature is 16–21°C (61–70°F), which, although an acceptable parameter for all species of cacti and succulents, can confuse both the plant and owner regarding whether to water or not. Despite the substrate drying out quickly due to evaporation caused by central heating, it isn't recommended to continue watering cacti and succulents often during dormant cold periods. The combination of the elevated temperature telling the plant to grow and the lack of light telling it "woah" can cause weak, spindly growth, known as etiolation, so it's better to place the plant next to a window in a cool room and drastically reduce watering to only once or twice during this period, to allow it to rest until more favourable conditions return. Forest cacti are the exception, which need water throughout cooler seasons, though not as frequently as in spring and summer.

Plant hardiness

Many cacti and succulents can survive low temperatures. How low varies from species to species, based on what they are used to in their native environment. Different organizations across the world have developed their own systems by which to classify a plant's hardiness.

USA

The USDA (United States Department of Agriculture) Hardiness Zone Map is used to classify geographic areas in the United States based on average annual minimum winter temperatures. The map divides the US into numbered zones, each representing a 10°F difference in temperature, from Zone 1, the coldest, to Zone 13, the warmest. The main zones are further divided into "a" and "b" sub-zones with a 5°F difference between them. This system, although not universally helpful, determines which plants are most likely to survive in a particular region.Its major drawback is that it doesn't consider other climatic conditions.
Many other factors besides minimum temperature determine whether or not a plant can survive in a given zone, such as humidity, rainfall, snow cover, or summer heat. Zone information alone is often inadequate for predicting winter survival, so use USDA zones only as a rough guide.

***Echinopsis lageniformis*, a desert-dwelling cactus native to Bolivia, will thrive in the heat of full sun.**

UK

USDA zones don't translate particularly well to the UK because they are designed for continental and subtropical climates. The UK has a weaker UV intensity because of its higher latitude, and also has cooler summers and damper conditions compared to the majority of the US. The combination of cold and damp can be disastrous for cacti and succulents. In 2012, the RHS introduced a hardiness rating system similar to the method used by the USDA, but it is organized differently, ranging from H1 (H stands for hardiness) for the most tender plants to H7 for the hardiest. In the UK, H1 refers to plants that can only survive here if grown in a heated greenhouse.

Australia

The Australian National Botanic Gardens devised a system of hardiness defined in steps of 5°C from −15°C to −10°C for Zone 1 to 15–20°C for Zone 7. Numerically, they are represented as being roughly six zones lower than the USDA system. For example, Australian Zone 3 is almost equivalent to USDA Zone 9.

Humidity

Humidity is an environmental factor linked to temperature that cannot be ignored when discussing optimum conditions for different species of cacti and succulents. The standard advice not to put them in a bathroom is based on the understanding that all succulent plants come from areas with dry air and therefore can't tolerate raised humidity levels. While this is true of some species, they don't all come from deserts. Cacti and succulents inhabit diverse environments, some of which can have oppressively high humidity. A bathroom is undoubtedly a suitable place for many species of forest-dwelling cacti (see page 148) as long as adequate light is provided.

Conversely, plants native to arid habitats can suffer if exposed to humidity much higher than they are used to, particularly in winter. Indoors, an average humidity reading ranges between 30–60 per cent, which is acceptable for most species of cacti and succulents. If it reaches above 70–80 per cent, however, ensure good air circulation to reduce excessive moisture by opening windows. In very humid climates, it can be beneficial to use a dehumidifier to maintain optimal growing conditions and reduce the risk of fungal disease and rot. The same rules of ventilation and airflow apply to conservatories and greenhouses.

If you're keen to monitor humidity, invest in a hygrometer, but bear in mind that as long as plants are grown in a free-draining substrate and receive the optimum intensity of sunlight and good airflow, you shouldn't need to worry about high humidity.

Though adapted to heat, arid cacti need good ventilation under glass to guard against humidity.

Understanding pH

If you are serious about giving your plants the best conditions, it is important to understand how pH level can impact their health. The pH scale measures the acidity or alkalinity of a substance, ranging from 0 to 14, with 7 being neutral, below 7 acidic, and above 7 alkaline.

At high pH levels, essential nutrients like iron, manganese, zinc, and phosphorus become less available to plants. Symptoms vary but can include yellowing (chlorosis), stunted growth, problems with flowering and, in worst-case scenarios, the death of the plant. The optimal pH range for most cacti and succulents is a slightly acidic value between 5 and 6.5.

The pH variables

Various factors can affect the stability of pH levels:

Substrate

Sandy soils usually have a lower pH; clay soils tend to have a higher pH. Organic matter tends to increase acidity as it decomposes. Beneficial soil microbes play a crucial role in nutrient cycling, and they thrive in a slightly acidic to neutral pH range. Most bagged cactus substrates are sterilized to prevent pathogens, which also eliminates these microbes, so it's recommended to add microbial inoculants.

Fertilizer

Fertilizers formulated for cacti and other succulent plants are generally designed to keep the substrate pH balanced, but it can change if you don't follow the application instructions carefully, potentially leading to an overaccumulation of minerals, which can cause "root burn" – dehydration by excessive salts. Look for a fertilizer that is pH buffered, as this can help mitigate issues and promote healthier growth.

Water

Hard tap water contains high levels of calcium and magnesium. When used over a long period, these can accumulate in the soil, increasing its alkalinity, so it's best to use rainwater whenever possible, as it's slightly acidic. If tap water is the only option, it's worth investing in a pH testing kit to know precisely how acidic or alkaline it is (see below).

How to test pH levels

To avoid problems, occasional pH testing is a good idea. Test strips are simple and inexpensive and give a general indication. For more accurate readings, electronic meters and soil-testing kits are available from garden centres or online.

Follow the steps below to test the pH level of water.

1. Use a clean container to collect the water you use for watering your cacti.
2. Dip a pH test strip or litmus paper into the water.
3. Compare the strip's colour to the chart to determine the water pH.

Most cacti and succulents need a slightly acidic pH level of 5–6.5 to thrive and flower like this *Mammillaria spinosissima*.

How to adjust pH

To lower the pH level in the garden, dig ericaceous compost into the soil or add sulphur. To raise the pH, use finely powdered limestone. Ericaceous compost can also be used as a base for a potting mix for indoor cacti and succulents to help counteract the alkalinity of hard tap water. To adjust the pH of tap water, use white vinegar or citric acid to lower it and bicarbonate of soda to raise it.

When adjusting pH you must do it slowly! Sudden changes can alter the availability of nutrients in the soil and disrupt beneficial microbes. Always raise or lower the pH in small increments over a few weeks to avoid shocking the plant.

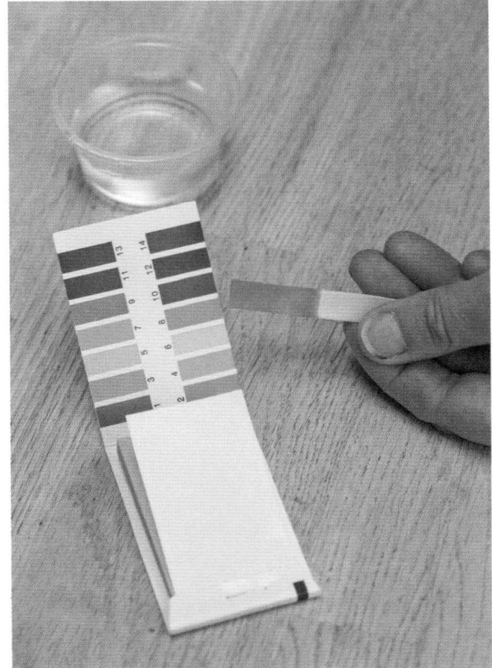

Test the pH of the water you use for your plants with litmus paper strips and a colour chart.

Fertilizer

You may have heard that you shouldn't feed cacti or succulents frequently, or even at all. Or, if you do, it must be with a specialist plant feed diluted to half-strength. While that's not entirely correct, there is some truth in it. You should proceed with caution when it comes to fertilizer.

All plants require essential nutrients, but not all require the same nutrient ratio. Cacti and other succulents need a slightly different ratio to other plants, which is informed by the soil in their native habitat.

Nutritional needs

Plant nutrients are split into macronutrients and micronutrients. As the name implies, plants need macronutrients in higher volumes than micronutrients. Nitrogen, phosphorus, and potassium are among the most significant macronutrients for plants. Micronutrients consist of iron, zinc, manganese, and copper (among others). The amounts needed varies from species to species, informed by what is available in their native habitat. Nitrogen, present in soils rich in organic matter, contributes to the structure of plant tissues. Phosphorus is primarily known for its role in promoting root development, flowering, and seed formation. Among other vital functions, potassium helps with the opening and closing of stomata, which is essential for photosynthesis, while magnesium is the building block for the green stuff, chlorophyll.

Key to knowing what feed to use and how often is understanding the environment in which the plant lives in the wild. A forest-dwelling, epiphytic cactus, like *Rhipsalis* (see page 166), comes from a very different habitat to an *Ariocarpus* (see page 106) and therefore has different requirements when it comes to substrate, frequency of watering, and fertilizing. The scant rainfall in deserts and other arid habitats means much of the soil is almost devoid of decaying organic matter. In contrast, forest cacti grow on branches or clamber over rocks rich in decomposing forest detritus. By recognizing these differences, you can better understand their specific nutritional needs.

Tailored solutions

Cacti and other succulent plants from habitats with xeric soil have adapted to nutrient-scarce environments that are particularly low in nitrogen, so it makes sense to use a specialist fertilizer with a lower nitrogen content, but which is high in phosphorus and potassium to encourage growth and flowers. Too much nitrogen can lead to lush, weak growth, which is more prone to stress and disease.

Epiphytic cacti from forest-like habitats rely on natural microorganisms and decaying organic matter to acquire nutrients, making them perfect candidates for fostering symbiotic relationships with beneficial fungi and microbes in your potting mix. They appreciate a fertilizer with an even NPK (nitrogen-phosphorus-potassium) ratio, replicating the nutrients available in their natural environment.

A fertilizer that is tailored to the nutrient needs of your plants will ensure abundant, productive growth.

Choosing your fertilizer

What you use to grow your plants can be more than just a substrate to hold the roots. Nurturing a community of microscopic allies to work harmoniously with your plant's roots, which aid nutrient absorption and overall plant health, should be the goal (see page 26). To support this microbial alliance, consider the following pros and cons when choosing fertilizers.

Organic fertilizers feed hungry plants while also supporting microbial systems.

Organic fertilizers

Pros They help support soil microbes while providing slow, steady nutrition.

Cons They work more gradually compared to synthetic fertilizers. However, this slow release of nutrients could be seen to mimic the cactus's adaptation to nutrient-scarce environments. Being composed of long-chain molecules, they require microbial action to break them down, making the nutrients available to the plant.

Synthetic liquid fertilizers can be tailored to specific plants' needs.

Synthetic liquid fertilizers

(Those that don't support microbial life; those that do will say so on the label.)

Pros These are easy to apply, quickly absorbed by the roots, and come in various ratios of NPK to cater to specific plant needs.

Cons Overuse can lead to the build-up of salts, causing osmotic dehydration.

Granular, slow-release fertilizers

Pros These provide nutrients over an extended period, reducing the need for frequent feeding.

Cons It is hard to apply granules evenly, and an excessive build-up can occur if not used carefully.

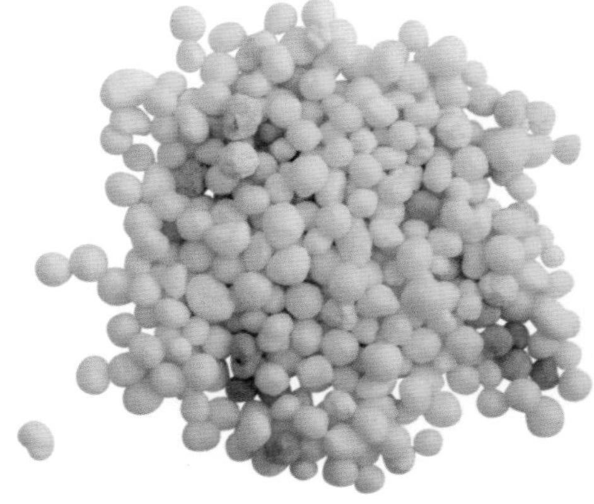

Granular fertilizers are slow-release, reducing the need for regular feeding.

Good-quality compost and vermicompost (worm poo)

Pros Rich in organic matter and microorganisms, compost and vermicompost contribute to healthy soil and encourage the development of beneficial microbes in your plant's root zone.

Cons Preparing and sourcing quality compost or vermicompost requires effort, but the soil fertility and microbial activity rewards are great.

Beneficial microbial inoculants

Pros These innovative fertilizers contain beneficial fungi and microbes that promote nutrient cycling, enhance the soil's structure, and bolster the health of plants.
Cons They might be slightly more expensive than conventional fertilizers, but the long-term benefits to your cactus habitat and its overall health make them a worthwhile investment.

Monitoring pH levels

The fertilizer you choose and the water you dilute it with can greatly impact the substrate pH and the microbial life within it. Synthetic fertilizers often contain ammonium or nitrate ions, which over time can make the substrate more acidic, while organic fertilizers and some slow-release formulas tend to have a more neutral or alkaline effect. Tap water, meanwhile, often contains dissolved minerals like calcium and magnesium, which can make the soil's pH more alkaline over time. By contrast, rainwater is naturally slightly acidic, making it ideal for cacti and succulents, which generally prefer mildly acidic conditions for optimal nutrient uptake.

Substrates that become too acidic or too alkaline, however, can lead to issues for your plants, reducing the availability of essential micronutrients – which can lead to symptoms like yellowing (chlorosis) and reduced growth – and harming beneficial soil microorganisms, reducing their population and activity. These microbes play a vital role in breaking down organic matter and cycling nutrients, so when their activity slows, even fewer nutrients become available to plants. Aim for a pH between 5 and 6.5 for most cacti and succulents, and check the soil's pH regularly to keep plants healthy (see page 56).

For those who want a deeper dive into plant care, testing the substrate periodically to assess pH can be interesting. Regular monitoring can help you make adjustments, so you can provide the best conditions for both the plant and the army of microscopic helpers that contribute to their wellbeing.

Compost and vermicompost are enriched with broken-down organic matter

Microbial inoculants contain living organisms to boost nutrient cycling.

Choosing a container

The choice of container can not only elevate a plant's appearance, but also affect its health. As well as aesthetics, materials and the practicalities of weight, moisture retention, and drainage should all be factored in to your decision.

Plastic or clay?

Both plastic and clay pots have pros and cons, and the choice of which to use should be informed by the plant's specific needs before aesthetic appeal, although ideally it would encompass both. Below are some factors to help you decide which is best for you.

	PLASTIC	CLAY
Pros	• Plastic retains moisture better than clay, so you may not need to water your plant as frequently. • It's generally cheaper than clay pots. • It is much lighter than clay, making it easier to move big plants. • It provides some degree of insulation, protecting plant roots from the most extreme temperatures.	• Clay is porous, which allows better airflow to the roots. • It looks more natural than plastic and comes in a variety of standard and unusual shapes. • In windy conditions, a clay pot is far less likely to topple over than plastic. It also provides more stability for top-heavy plants.
Cons	• The moisture retention of plastic leaves a greater margin for error when it comes to watering. • It doesn't provide as much aeration to the roots as clay. • Cheap plastic degrades over time when exposed to sunlight, which can cause pots to become brittle and break. • Tall plants or those that overhang can become unstable in a lightweight pot.	• Clay absorbs water, making the substrate dry out faster, which can mean having to water more frequently. • Large clay pots can be challenging to move around. • Clay pots are more expensive than plastic ones. • Clay can be easily smashed (though broken shards can be used to cover large drainage holes).

Be creative with your container choice, as well as considering practical matters such as the pot material and drainage holes.

Decorative pots

Charity shops and reclamation yards are a great place to find cheap and unusual pots to complement your plant collection. A unique-looking pot combined with a fascinating plant can have double the impact, making a stylish statement in your home or garden. Experiment with height by potting trailing plants into vintage jardinières or wall-hanging planters.

How to drill drainage holes into containers

It is always preferable to pot up plants into a container with existing drainage holes to allow excess water to escape. However, don't discount a container because it doesn't have a drainage hole, as it's simple to drill one.

Equipment

Safety goggles

Broken ceramics (optional)

A drill

A masonry drill bit for unglazed surfaces/a glass and tile drill bit for glazed ceramic planters

Masking tape

1 Put on the safety googles. If you've never tried this before, practise first on some broken ceramic tiles or pottery.

2 Place the container upside down on a piece of wood so it doesn't slip. Fit the drill with the correct bit for the material you are drilling into. If it's a glazed container, stick strips of masking tape where you want the holes to be so the drill bit doesn't slip.

3 Set the drill speed to low and slowly make a few holes in the base. If the drill bit heats up while making the hole, pour some water into the drilled area. To avoid cracking the base, don't apply too much pressure, particularly with glazed containers.

Potting

As with any other plant, cacti and succulents need to be repotted into a larger container so their growth isn't inhibited and they don't become pot-bound. A common misconception is that because some of these plants have a shallow root system, they shouldn't need repotting, but if a plant is growing, assume that its root system is also growing.

When plant roots outgrow their pot, the substrate can no longer supply what's needed for good growth. There might be no overt signs of distress, but all such plants will benefit from being transferred to a larger container.

A larger pot, however, should not be *too* big for the roots. Pouring water into a large pot of soil, when the roots take up only a small proportion of that area, increases the risk of the soil staying wet for a prolonged period, leading to root rot, so it's best to go up only one or two pot sizes.

Plants that are repotted when they outgrow their container can reach impressive sizes.

Signs that your plant needs repotting

Look out for the following telltale signs that your plant has outgrown its pot:

- Roots growing out of the drainage holes.
- There hasn't been any visible growth for a long time.
- The plant looks too big for the pot or looks unbalanced.
- The pot is distorting out of shape.

If you notice any of these signs, it's time to investigate further by looking at the roots themselves. If the plant has spines, wrap a piece of cardboard around it to gently remove it from the pot. If it won't come out easily, lay it on its side and press on the pot a few times to loosen it, then pull out the plant gently. You should be able to see if the roots need more room to grow.

This is also a good opportunity to check the health of the roots and to examine the plant for any signs of pests such as root mealybugs (see page 96). If the potting mix falls away but the roots don't need a larger pot, the plant can go back into the same pot with fresh substrate. If the roots are circling around the pot, the plant should be repotted into a larger one.

How to repot

Cacti and other succulent plants can be tricky to repot because of spines or spreading growth habits. This method avoids injury or soil getting onto the plant.

1 Find a clean pot one or two sizes larger than the current one. If the plant has spines, wrap cardboard around it, and gently remove it from its pot. If the root ball is a solid mass, gently free some of the outer roots with your fingers.

2 Add some potting mix to the larger pot. Place the old pot inside the new one and push down gently.

3 Fill the gap between the pots with potting mix, pressing it firmly down as you go. Then remove the inner pot to leave a pot-shaped hole.

4 Pick up the plant (still with cardboard around the stem) and put it carefully into the hole in the new pot.

5 Add more potting mix if necessary and gently press down to ensure the plant stands upright.

6 Add decorative grit to the surface if desired.

It's tempting to water the plant straight after repotting, but it should be left for at least a week before doing so, to give any roots that might have been damaged a chance to heal.

Repot new plants

Commercial growers often use the same substrate for tropical plants as they do for cacti and succulents, which can be too water-retentive. Or, when you buy an epiphyte (such as the Easter cactus below) they are often potted up in coir, which can become hydrophobic. For healthy roots, it's best to repot into a more suitable potting mix.

1 Gently remove the new plant from the pot it was bought in.

2 Using your fingers, get rid of as much of the old substrate as possible.

3 Mix together a new substrate of 50 per cent potting compost, with 50 per cent fir bark (used for potting orchids) and perlite or vermiculite.

4 Add a little of the potting mix to the bottom of a new pot, place the plant in, and fill in around the sides.

1

2

3

4

When to repot

There is conflicting advice about the best time of year to repot cacti and succulents. If a plant is in obvious distress, my advice would be to attend to it regardless of the season, as it could make the difference between life and death. However, if you live in a country with cold winters, avoid repotting during this period and wait until spring.

Cleaning

Dust accumulates on the surface of plants, making them look dull and unattractive, but more importantly it can negatively impact their growth, so while cleaning them can restore their natural beauty, it's their health that is improved after a spa session.

Dust cacti stems lightly with a paintbrush to remove debris that can hinder photosynthesis.

Why clean your plants?

A layer of dust on leaves – or stems in the case of cacti – can hinder photosynthesis by blocking sunlight from reaching the plant's surface, impeding its ability to produce energy, grow, and thrive. Dust and debris on the surface can also create a very welcoming environment for pests and pathogens, which can potentially lead to infestations or diseases. Airflow, which is essential for the gas-exchange element of photosynthesis, can also be restricted by a layer of dust clogging the stomata, affecting respiration.

How to clean your plants

While the leaves of succulent plants, with some exceptions, are mostly free from spines or thorns, and can therefore simply be wiped with a damp cloth or sponge to remove dust, cacti are a little more challenging. Wiping a stem covered with vicious spines isn't going to work, but a paintbrush, toothbrush, or hand-held hoover with a brush attachment for larger species are very effective in removing dust and cobwebs.

A small artist's paintbrush is perfect for getting into the nooks and crannies, while a toothbrush is very useful on columnar species covered in spines such as *Weberbauerocereus* or *Trichocereus*. Alternatively, if you have outside space, take the plants outside and give them a spray with the hose. Always be gentle and take care when cleaning plants so as not to damage the cuticle or spines.

For spikier plants that are difficult to clean, give them an occasional spray-wash with a hose.

Heirloom plants

To some, plants are far more than decorative objects. They can evoke a deep emotional attachment, particularly if they previously belonged to a loved one. Like a piece of jewellery or a trinket, a plant can be a family heirloom.

This emotional connection we make with plants is something I find fascinating. In early 2024, I went to collect a very old *Cleistocactus strausii* (see page 116) from a home in Bournemouth. Very sadly, the owner had passed away, and his daughter had got in touch asking if I would take care of it, as she had no room for it herself. We drove to collect the cactus and discovered that it had been given as a wedding present to her great-grandparents and then been passed down through the generations, making the plant between 120 and 150 years old.

The cactus hadn't been repotted in decades and was much smaller than one would expect for such an old plant, but it had so much character and history that I couldn't help but fall in love with it. To imagine that it has lived through two world wars is quite something. Although it has no personal connection to me, I feel honoured to be its custodian.

So I would urge you, before buying a new plant, to see if you can rehome an old one. Search online societies and second-hand websites, or visit house-clearance sales, to see if you can find old plants in need of a new home. I feel passionately that rescuing heirloom plants is important to preserve the memory of the owner, and the plant, for future generations.

Sara Blanchard's huge, 80-year-old Christmas cactus is a magnificent specimen that links her to her grandmother, Eloise.

Sara Blanchard's Christmas cactus

Sara Blanchard is the caretaker of an extraordinary family heirloom.

Name **Sara Blanchard**

Location **South Burlington, Vermont**

Tell us about your Christmas cactus.
The cactus was owned by my mother's mother, Eloise Conrad, who started it from a clipping of her sister's plant in 1943. When Granny Eloise went into a nursing home we moved her 60-year-old Christmas cactus, which I now call "Granny", to my house. It has always been the centre of attention because of its size and beautiful fuchsia-coloured flowers, which always bloom from December through until May.

Why is it special to you?
I have always loved the plant and have fond memories of my parents helping Eloise repot it when it got too large for its pot, and of her letting me water it when I was a child.

How do you care for it?
I water "Granny" from the top, 3.75 litres (1 gallon) every 10 to 14 days, and add a flower-boosting fertilizer once a month. When we repot, I use a specialist succulent and cactus soil mix. I layer the bottom with small stones for drainage, pour some soil in the pot, then break the old ceramic pot to get it out. I loosen up the root ball and then four people lift the plant and put it into the new pot. I add some soil to the top, then water it. "Granny" lives in my sunroom and gets some south, south-west, and west sun, but not enough to burn the cladodes. She turned 80 last year and is currently almost 1.2 metres (4ft) wide.

Propagation

A cost-effective way to boost your collection, replicate plants you love, and advance your growing skills, propagation is a hugely rewarding process. Discover the joy of nurturing a tiny seed or cutting and watching it grow into a mature, blooming plant.

Propagating from seed

Although it takes longer than propagating from a cutting, and the success rate can be unpredictable, there are many reasons to give growing from seeds a go:

- Buying seeds is far cheaper than buying new plants.
- You get to enjoy watching a plant grow.
- You'll have multiple plants that can be traded with others or given as gifts.
- It's easier to find specialist varieties that are not available as plants.

Propagating cacti and other succulents from seed can be done at any time of year, but if you live in a country with cold winters (unless you use a heat mat under your seed trays to gently warm the soil), it's best to wait until spring. You might find it surprising, given their native habitat, but cacti and succulent seeds need a constantly moist environment and don't like strong direct sunlight.

SEED COLLECTION

Collecting seeds from your own plant saves money and allows you to preserve and propagate unique or heirloom plants. Once your cacti or succulent has flowered and the seed pods are fully mature and dry, carefully remove them from the plant. To extract the seeds gently open the pods over a clean, flat surface. You may need to use tweezers or a toothpick if the seeds are tiny. Some pods may contain a pulp; if so, rinse the seeds to separate them. Lay the seeds on a piece of kitchen towel and let them dry for a few days, then store in a labelled envelope or container until you're ready to sow them.

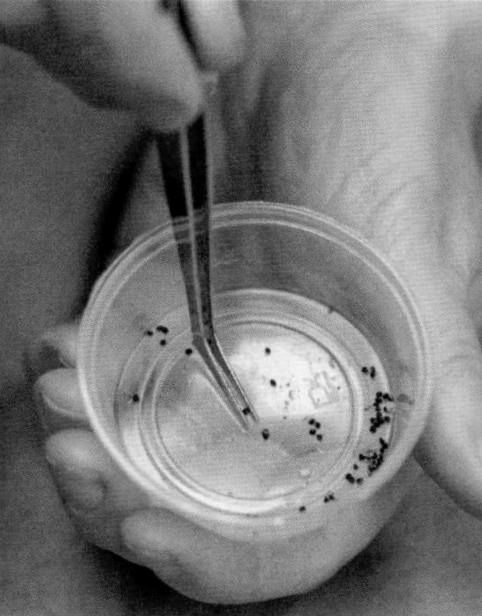

Tweezers can be used to extract pods from the parent plant and seeds from within the pods.

How to sow seeds

There are many different methods for growing from seed. This one works for me.

Equipment

Potting compost

A microwavable bowl (optional)

Spray bottle filled with water (preferably distilled tap water or rainwater)

Small pots or clear plastic takeaway containers with lids

Perlite

Seeds

Clear plastic food bags

Labels

Heat mat (optional)

Before you start

It's good practice to sterilize the compost before sowing to eradicate fungal spores and microscopic insect eggs, which can be present in commercial soils. Scoop the compost into a microwavable bowl, lightly spritz with water, and heat in the microwave for 2 minutes on full power. Alternatively, put the soil in an ovenproof dish, cover with foil, and heat in the oven at 82°C (180°F) for 30 minutes. Allow to cool in the bowl or dish before using.

1

2

3

1 Add the cooled compost to a pot or plastic takeaway container along with some perlite to create a 50:50 mix.

2 Spritz the potting mix with water to dampen it.

3 Sow the seeds evenly on the surface. I find it easier to pour the seeds into the palm of my hand and use my fingers to pinch and scatter them over the compost surface. There's no need to cover the seeds with extra compost. (Steps continue overleaf.)

Tip

Soaking your seeds in water overnight before you sow them can improve the germination rate of certain species, but do check the seed packet instructions first.

4 Put the lid on the container. If using a pot, seal it in a clear plastic bag to prevent moisture from escaping and pathogens from entering. Label the seeds.

5 Position the container or pot in a warm, bright place. A windowsill is ideal, but if it gets direct sunlight, provide some shading. An optimum temperature for germination is around 21°C (70°F). In cold weather this can be achieved by placing a heat mat under the pots.

6 Germination takes 7–21 days if conditions are perfect. It's important that the substrate doesn't dry out; if the container is kept sealed the condensation should keep the seeds moist, but do stay vigilant and spritz with water if needed.

AFTERCARE

When your plants are nine to twelve months old you can slowly start to acclimatize them to the open air. Open the the container lid or the bag for longer periods of time over a few weeks until the coverings are permanently removed. Keep spraying the substrate so it doesn't fully dry out. When the plants are beginning to look like they're getting too big for their pot (this can be anywhere from six months to two years, depending on the species) move them into individual pots with free-draining potting mix.

Propagate from leaf cuttings

Most succulent plants with thick, juicy leaves can be propagated from a single leaf.

1

1 Gently pull a leaf from the plant with your fingers. The leaf needs to come away from the stem fully intact. Set aside for 24 hours to let the end callous over.

2 Fill a pot with free-draining potting mix. Then spritz the substrate with water.

3 Lay the leaf on the surface of the substrate, then place the pot on a warm windowsill, out of direct sunlight.

Equipment

A leafy succulent plant

Small pot

Free-draining potting mix (see page 44)

Spray bottle filled with water (preferably distilled tap water or rainwater)

2

3

AFTERCARE

The leaf will grow roots within two to three weeks, after which a small plant will develop at the end. There is no need to remove the old leaf as it will naturally shrivel and die.

Propagate from stem cuttings

Succulent stems are easy to propagate, but it's important to allow the cut end to callous over before planting to reduce the likelihood of disease and rot.

Equipment

Scissors or a sharp knife

Surgical spirit (rubbing alcohol)

Kitchen paper

A cactus or succulent with multiple stems or offsets (young plants)

A suitable-sized pot for the cutting

Free-draining potting mix (see page 44)

Spray bottle filled with water (preferably distilled water or rainwater)

1 Clean your scissors or knife with surgical spirit (rubbing alcohol) using a sheet of kitchen paper.

2 Cut off an offset or stem from the plant. Set it aside until the cut has calloused over – this can take a few days or more than a week depending on the thickness of the stem.

3 Some plants, like members of the *Euphorbia* family, have a milky latex that will seep out after cutting the stem. To stop the flow, dip the cut end into water.

1

2

3

Tip

A large cutting may need support. Secure it to a stick or cane twice its length using plant Velcro tape or string, so the top of it is halfway down the stick, then push the cane into the substrate so that the cut end of the stem is a little way into the substrate.

4 Fill a pot with free-draining potting mix. Then spray the substrate lightly with water.

5 Depending on the size of the stem or offset, the cut end can be pushed a little way into the substrate.

AFTERCARE

Keep the cutting out of direct sunlight and allow the substrate to dry out before spraying with water again. Depending on the size, the cutting or offset should grow roots within a few weeks or months. Larger cuttings can take longer.

How to graft

Grafting fuses two separate plants so they grow as one, the bottom part providing water, food, and nutrients to the cutting on top. The technique is used to propagate hard-to-grow species, rescue a damaged plant, or facilitate the cultivation of plants that would not survive on their own.

Equipment

Tissue

Surgical spirit (rubbing alcohol)

Craft knife with sharp blade

Rootstock plant (here, *Hylocereus trigonus;* the following strong growers also work well:

Harrisia jusbertii

Mammillaria bocasana

Myrtillocactus geometrizans

Soehrensia spachiana)

Scion plant (here, *Parodia*)

Small piece of cardboard

Rubber bands

Grafting terms

Vascular bundle The circular core of each stem, through which water, food, and nutrients travel

Xylem Tissue carrying water and minerals up from roots

Phloem Tissue carrying glucose and amino acids downwards

Scion A cutting from the plant you want to grow on

Rootstock The host plant onto which the scion is grafted; it should be a sturdy, healthy, vigorous grower

1 Before you start, use a tissue soaked in surgical spirit to carefully clean and sterilize both sides of the craft knife blade to prevent diseases being introduced to the cut surfaces. Then cut the top off the rootstock plant with the knife, cutting cleanly and straight to leave as flat a surface as possible. Examine the inside of the stem: it should be fresh and juicy, with no discoloration.

2 Next, chamfer – cut at a roughly 45-degree angle – the ends of each rib of the rootstock. Making slopes on each rib is important to stop the cut surface from shrinking and becoming hollow as it dries.

3 Cut a very thin sliver across the top of the rootstock and leave it in place. Forming a sliver ensures the cut remains completely clean and wet until you're ready to make the graft.

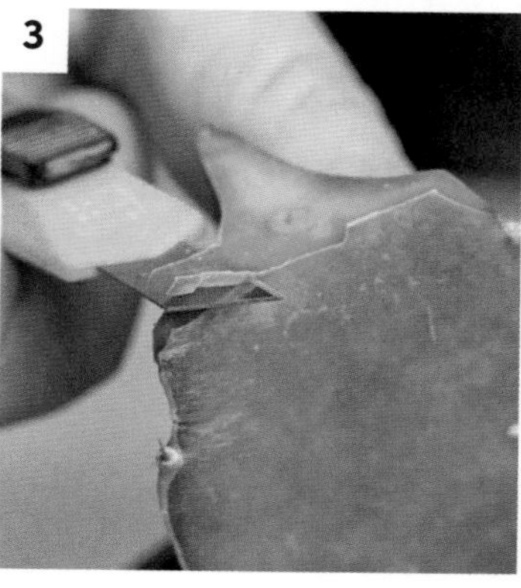

4 Now it's time to prepare the scion to be placed on top. Clean the blade as before and cut off the piece for grafting. Again, make sure the cutting is healthy with no signs of discoloration. As with the rootstock, cut another thin sliver and leave it in place. Protect your fingers from any spines with a piece of cardboard.

5 Remove the thin slices from both rootstock and scion. Before placing the scion, look carefully at both vascular bundles and try to line up the rings as best you can. If the bundles are significantly different in size, make sure they cross one another, or the graft will fail. Try to avoid any air bubbles being trapped by gently turning and pressing them together.

6 To hold the graft in place, stretch two rubber bands over the top of the cutting and under the pot, at 90 degrees to each other.

Tip

Don't throw away the remnants of the grafted plants. Let the top piece of the rootstock callous over and replant it to use again for grafting once it has developed a healthy root system.

AFTERCARE

Keep the pot somewhere warm but not in direct sunlight, and do not water for a few weeks. Protect from full sun until it's clear the scion has taken to the rootstock: look for new growth or signs of the scion plumping up. A flaccid scion means that, though it may have adhered to the rootstock, it might not be getting any water and therefore the graft failed. Grafting can require practice, as success depends on many factors, but it is worth persevering! Once there are obvious signs that the graft has been successful, you can water it as normal and treat it like any other plant in your collection.

Creating an indoor garden

With our increasing reliance on technology, we now spend the majority of our lives indoors and find it increasingly hard to connect with nature. So why not bring nature indoors?

Greening up your interior has numerous benefits, both aesthetically and for your mental wellbeing. Plants can calm an overactive brain, reduce stress, and improve mood, while also making a home look more inviting. Before you start cramming plants into every available space, however, it's important to acknowledge that they are living organisms with basic needs, which must be considered first.

Light

Without light, a once-beautiful specimen can be reduced to a mound of desiccated brown cells or a rotting pool of gunge – not a design statement anyone sets out to create. Therefore, the first rule of plant styling must be light. Start by assessing the areas in your home that receive the most natural light. Unless you are prepared to buy grow lights (see page 40), next to a window is where you should imagine your interior landscape.

The right plant

During winter, many of us rely on central heating or take off to warmer climates. Luckily, cacti and succulents laugh in the face of radiators and can be left unwatered for weeks, making them ideal for warm, dry homes and busy lifestyles. However, choose carefully. Most species need bright, direct sunlight to thrive, but some prefer to be close to a window yet out of direct sun. See Chapter 3 (page 100) for help choosing.

Display options

Windowsills are the obvious place to grow plants, but you don't need to stick to this area. Try epiphytic cacti in hanging planters so the entire window becomes like a living forest. Add visual interest by playing with height and shape, placing taller succulents with smaller globular cacti to create a more natural display. You can also use tall stands to raise plants off the floor, so they reach the window.

If you're lucky enough to have a conservatory, you can create your own indoor botanical garden, utilizing the floor, adjoining wall, and ceiling to create a tranquil oasis. Hanging trailing plants from the ceiling will show them off to their full potential while also providing them with the ideal light intensity and making use of all your available space, giving the feeling of being immersed in a jungle.

Shelves and worktops can be useful to lift the plants off the ground and make them a focal point of the room. Or you can try using greenhouse staging for a tiered display. I also love seeing old pieces of furniture repurposed to show off plants. A dresser with plants spilling out of the drawers and draped with epiphytes can make a unique talking point.

Design considerations

Think like a gardener when it comes to designing your interior space. Once you've considered light requirements, you can unleash your inner artist. Here are some key points to think about:

- **Scale and proportion** Pay attention to the size of plants and containers relative to the space they occupy to avoid ending up with overcrowded or underwhelming plant arrangements.
- **Accessories** Choose pots that complement the style of the plants without overshadowing them. For a unique look, choose vintage or antique.
- **Create a focal point** Use larger or more striking plants, unusual containers, or creative displays to highlight a particular area of the room.
- **Asymmetry** Symmetrical arrangements convey a sense of order and formality but can look too uptight. Grouping plants in uneven numbers looks more natural.
- **Superabundance** If you prefer the maximalist approach, you can use an almost excessive number of plants to create a lush, immersive space. When done right it can be stunning.

Find unusual ways to display your plants – on shelves (top left), spilling out of drawers (top right), or crammed into every nook and cranny for a superabundant look (right).

Make a dish garden

An interesting way to show off plants indoors is to make a planted display in a bowl. It's best not to mix cacti and other succulents in the same bowl, as they often have different care requirements, but that's not to say you can't make one of each.

Don't overfill the bowl as it might inhibit growth. Start by selecting three or five plants if the bowl is large enough, and consider using specimens of different heights and shapes. Globular cacti such as *Mammillaria*, *Rebutia*, and *Echinopsis* are a good choice for low-growing plants. If planting a succulent bowl, add in *Sedum morganianum* or *Curio rowleyanus* to crawl between *Echeveria* or *Aloe aristata* and cascade over the sides. I advise using a larger bowl for succulents than for cacti.

1 Start by selecting a suitable container. If it doesn't have drainage holes, either drill some into the bottom (see page 63) or add a layer of clay shards or clay balls to the base.

2 Mix together a suitable free-draining potting mix (see page 44) and add a shallow layer to the bowl.

3 Gently remove some of the soil from the outer roots of your chosen plants, then place them in the bowl, moving them around until you are happy with how they look.

4 Fill in around the plants with potting mix and gently press down until they stand upright without toppling over.

5 Decorate the surface with small pebbles or rocks if desired. Dust off any excess with a small paintbrush to keep the plants looking neat.

6 Place the bowl on a bright windowsill or in a conservatory.

7 Wait about a week or so and then water around the plants' roots. Be extra-careful not to water too much if your dish does not have drainage holes.

Bonsai succulents

Wide, shallow dishes are ideal for showcasing the beauty of a single succulent, enabling you to recreate the look of the much-revered Japanese art of bonsai. Good plants to use are *Aichryson dichotomum*, *Ceraria namaquensis*, *Sedum frutescens* (also known as tree sedum), and *Crassula sarcocaulis*, a small shrubby succulent known by the common name bonsai crassula, because of its uncanny bonsai-like appearance.

The beauty of a bonsai tree is often in the trunk, which can be recreated by removing the lower leaves from a succulent with a woody stem. Caudiciform plants also look striking in a shallow pot with the woody caudex exposed.

In a shallow dish, it can be hard to ensure the plant stands upright. Bonsai pots usually have two holes at the bottom through which wire can be fed to hold the plant in place. Alternatively, place a rock on top of the substrate; this adds to the overall aesthetic and helps stop the plant from toppling over.

A single tree-like succulent, such as *Crassula sarcocaulis*, can be styled like a bonsai.

Grower profile

Steph Wilson & Tom Rapley

Location South London, UK

Specialism Propagation and styling

Photographer Steph and horticulturist Tom have created a unique and beautiful home, combining their love for plants, art, and antiques. Steph's eye for detail and innate ability to pair the right plant with the perfect pot has created an exceptional space, which has graced the pages of international design magazines.

What are your top tips for styling a home with plants?

Don't compromise with the easiest and quickest option by grabbing a pot from a generic home store or garden centre – it'll cheapen the plant and the space it's in. Scour flea markets, antique markets, eBay, Facebook Marketplace; commission friends who are ceramicists; go to pottery-studio sample sales – consider any vessel that catches your eye... If the pot is beautiful, it can be as impactful as the plant it holds (sometimes more so).

Which plant has been your best find?

The 6-metre (19¾ft) *Euphorbia* in the main space. I got it for £100 about five years ago when it was about a metre (3¼ft) shorter. It had outgrown someone's conservatory and was growing to the shape of its angled roof, which is still visible in the plant's shape now.

What's been your biggest failure?

Our 2.5-metre (8¼ft) *Euphorbia ramipressa,* which I overwatered, unknowingly rotting the roots, so it then fell over when I moved it, so I then firmed it back down and watered it again (help!), and by that point it was too far gone to propagate. Believe me, we tried. We learned that, when in doubt with succulents, it's better to underwater than overwater (especially during the darker months).

How do you deal with pests?

We remove pests by hand as much as we can and keep the plants free of dead leaves. Otherwise, we quarantine an infested plant in my studio, or even cut it right back and start again.

What advice would you give about watering during the different seasons?

Go lighter on watering in the winter. With cacti, as soon as it drops below around 18°C (64°F), we virtually stop watering altogether. You never want plants sitting in water for too long; they need to dry out a little or totally between watering. Don't create generic watering schedules. It really is down to observation of the soil, feeling how wet or dry it is, or simply lifting the pot – if it's heavy, it's holding water. If it's very light, it's dry.

What advice would you give beginners?

Trial a few plants without huge investment first – so many are up for "adoption" online, and will probably be more mature (and therefore harder to kill!). When feeling more confident, level up to a rarer, more expensive, and probably more vulnerable plant if you want to test your knowledge. Also, you can never do too much research, or ask enough questions. Any real plant lover will jump at the chance to give tips and advice!

What are your top tips for plant care?

Research, experiment, and be prepared for some losses for a good few years. Even when you think you've understood a plant's needs, there will always be a way that they can surprise you.

Xeriscaping

As stunning as they are indoors, cacti and other succulents really come into their own when grown outside. They grow faster, have more leaves or spines, and are more likely to flower. The next best thing to seeing them grow in habitat is creating your own landscaped garden where you can enjoy them – known as xeriscaping.

There are many benefits of growing xerophytes in the garden. Most are evergreen, drought tolerant, and need little in the way of pruning, deadheading, or feeding. They also make a dramatic addition to otherwise traditional gardens.

Things to consider

Before you rush out to buy a huge agave, it's essential to do some initial planning. Here is a list of important considerations for xeriscaping your garden:

1. Climatic conditions The most important factor. If you live in a hot, arid climate, there is an almost endless choice of cacti and succulents you can grow outside. In other parts of the world, great care needs to be taken to choose plants that can withstand wet and cold conditions. Research your geographical location both in broad terms (i.e. where in the country you live), but also whether you live in a town or open countryside. Towns are generally a degree or so warmer.
2. Location Cacti and succulents generally thrive in areas with plenty of sunlight. Mark the sunniest places of the garden on a piece of paper, bearing in mind that walls, fences, and hedges cast shadows.
3. Soil Cacti and succulents need free-draining soil. Dense soil must be amended with sand or grit to improve drainage and ensure a balance of organic and inorganic matter to at least a 50:50 ratio. Ericaceous compost and lime-free grit make a suitable substrate for most cacti and other succulent plants. Avoid areas with clay soil or those prone to standing water if planting directly into the ground. Raised beds or rockeries (see page 86) are an option in these areas. It's also wise to test soil pH and amend it if necessary before planting (see page 56).
4. Shelter Be aware of wind direction. Planting near a wall gives shelter and the stone or brick can act like a storage heater, which is beneficial in colder climates.
5. Size Measure your planting area so you know how many plants you can fit in.
6. Plant selection Check the hardiness of your plants (see page 54) and make a list of those that can tolerate living in your locality. From this list, choose cacti and succulents of different shapes, sizes, colours, and textures to create visual interest. Consider both tall and low-growing species, as well as those with striking flowers or architectural forms.
7. Design Finalize the layout of your garden on paper. Consider factors such as height, colour, texture, and growth habits when arranging your plants. Group those with similar requirements together.

A gravel garden of cacti and succulents interspersed with drought-tolerant annuals and perennials such as poppies and verbena looks stunning.

Preparing the ground

Once the soil has been prepared and any weeds removed, cover the area with a permeable weed-suppressing membrane. Before cutting into the membrane, position your plants on top and move them around until you like the overall design. As a general rule, large plants should be single and smaller plants should be grouped together in odd numbers of three or five so that the arrangement looks natural.

Planting

Once you're happy with the scheme, remove each plant from its pot and lay it on its side. Cut a cross in the membrane next to each plant, dig a hole beneath it a bit larger than the root ball, and position the plant in it. Fill in around the plant to stabilize it and ensure there are no air pockets. Firm in and, if the ground is dry, water in thoroughly before folding the membrane back into place. Once all the plants are in, cover the membrane with a topdressing of gravel.

Planters and containers

Plants can also be grown in borders, raised beds, fixed planters, or movable pots to add visual interest to an outdoor space or to grow plants that can't stay outside during the colder months. A good way to break up a featureless wall is to add planter boxes on top and let succulent plants trail down to soften the structure. Large pots – a big spiky agave, aloe, or opuntia in an old stone urn, for example – can create accents on patios or decking, or line an otherwise boring pathway. Source pots from reclamation yards and thrift stores to create your own unique style.

How to make a rockery

Rockeries, or rock gardens, have a long history in European garden design, and have evolved to suit a variety of styles and purposes. They are often used in xeriscaping as they are a good way to mimic the natural habitat of many cacti and succulent species, including those from alpine regions. To make your own rockery:

1 **Plan** Walk around the garden to find the best site. A rockery can add height to an otherwise flat garden or transform a difficult sloped area. Consider the size and shape of the plot, as well as whether there is enough sunlight to support the growth of xeric plants. A sloping, well-drained site is ideal.

2 **Prepare the site** Clear the area where you will be creating the rockery, removing any existing vegetation and debris. Then, add a layer of weed-suppressing membrane.

3 **Choose the rocks** Visually, it works best to choose one type of rock rather than a mishmash of different ones, but do look for rocks of different shapes and sizes to create visual interest and make the area look more natural.

4 **Arrange the rocks** Start with the biggest ones at the base and work your way up with smaller rocks. Experiment with different configurations until you're happy with the layout. Don't forget to leave large enough gaps between the rocks to plant your cacti and succulents.

5 **Add soil** Once you've arranged your rocks, fill in the gaps with a 50:50 mix of lime-free soil and either sand or grit.

6 **Choose your plants** Pick plants suitable for your local climate conditions. Consider a combination of low-growing alpine plants and succulents, as well as taller columnar cacti to add height.

7 **Arrange the plants** Position the plants among the rocks, taking into account their potential mature size. Once you're happy with the arrangement, remove them from their pots, cut a cross into the membrane, and plant them through it.

The beauty of a rockery is that it can be any size, taking up a whole garden, a sloping hillside, or just a small area. A mini-rockery can even be created in an old sink, tub, or bowl – just ensure there are drainage holes so it doesn't turn into a bog garden.

Grower profile

Paul Spracklin

Location Benfleet, Essex, UK

Specialism Gardening with cacti and succulents outside

Membership British Cactus and Succulent Society

Paul is a garden designer who has created what most would think impossible: a garden in the UK, full of cacti and succulents. Paul is author of *The Dry Exotic Garden* and gives talks and advice on xeric planting.

What inspired you to create a UK garden using cacti and succulents?

I became bitten by the exotic gardening bug in the mid-1980s, wanting to turn my garden into a jungle. However, I live in one of the driest parts of England, so after a few years it occurred to me I should look for plants that were just as exotic, but capable of withstanding my arid growing conditions. Then I saw an episode of the BBC's *Gardeners' World* when they visited Lotusland gardens in California, and that set me off on this adventure.

Which plant are you most proud of and why?

My standout is the very tall columnar cactus, *Trichocereus terscheckii,* which I planted in 2003 at 2.5 metres (8¼ft) high and is now nearly 5 metres (16½ft). I don't think there's another quite that size that has been in the ground that long. It took an enormous act of faith to invest in such a large plant, which then had little to no track record of being grown in the UK. To see it thrive is incredibly rewarding.

What substrate do you use for your plants?

Some of the more robust plants such as yuccas are fine in normal soil as long as it drains. But for pickier plants such as cacti and agaves, in raised borders and rockeries, I have migrated towards a completely inorganic substrate: rubble, crushed concrete and brick, all-in ballast, sharp sand.

How do you care for your plants outside through the seasons?

I only feed or water plants that I feel need to have their growth pushed along a bit. Otherwise, I tend to leave them all to fend for themselves, and they seem happy like that. Growing the plants hard like this makes them better prepared for the rigours of winter. At times I've covered some of the raised beds for winter to stop rain and snow settling on the plants, but I'm edging towards a pleasing mix of plants I can grow without a cover.

What advice would you give beginners on planting a cactus and succulent garden?

Find the sunniest spot you have. Unless your native soil is gravel or grit, plant into raised borders. Species choice is particularly important – it took a huge amount of research, followed by a huge amount of trial and error, for me to assemble a portfolio of suitable plants. Allow good air movement, and above all, don't be scared to try things.

Three plants everyone should grow?

1. ***Yucca linearifolia.*** Yuccas are key structural elements in xeric gardens, and this one is better suited to colder climates than most.
2. ***Agave ovatifolia.*** This species is moisture, cold, and heat tolerant. Not only that, it's drop-dead gorgeous.
3. ***Nolina hibernica.*** Hands down, the best trunking species of *Nolina* for colder climes.

Paul and his bed of large columnar cacti, including the giant *Trichocereus terscheckii*.

Various cacti and succulents thriving in the ground, planted into a large slope of rubble.

Columnar cactus
Denmoza rhodacantha

The prickly pear cactus
Opuntia scheeri

Troubleshooting

Although cacti and succulents are considered tough, like all plants they can be susceptible to problems. Some issues are unavoidable, but healthy plants are less likely to succumb to ailments or pest attacks than those under stress. It's always advisable to isolate new plants from the rest of your collection until you can be sure there are no signs of pests or disease, and to be extra-vigilant when caring for them. It is far easier to deal with a problem early than in the advanced stages.

Rotting

Symptoms Soft, mushy growth or roots, the plant has collapsed, and there may be fungus gnats crawling on the soil (see page 99).

Treatment Rotting is the most common problem cacti and other succulents face, particularly those kept indoors. It's usually caused by a combination of lack of light, too much water, and a non-free-draining substrate. There is no choice but to cut away the rot before it consumes the entire plant. If the rot has started at the base, cut away the plant above it and propagate it from stems (see page 74). If the rot is at the top, cut the top part away. Depending on the species, it may regrow from where the cut was made. If not, I'm afraid you will have to live with a permanently disfigured plant, but at least it's still alive!

Overwatering, a non-free-draining substrate, and lack of light are common causes of rot in cacti and succulents.

Nutrient deficiencies

Symptoms Stunted growth, chlorosis (pale or yellow leaves due to a lack of chlorophyll), overall paleness, browning of the growing point.

Treatment There is a misconception that because cacti and succulents come from places with nutritionally poor soil, they don't need fertilizer. They may not need feeding as often as other plants, but most – particularly those in pots – benefit from being fed once a month during the growing season.

Fungal disease

Symptoms Rust-coloured or black lesions on the stem or leaves.

Treatment Fungal infections are uncommon, but lack of airflow, high humidity, pests, overwatering, and plant damage can make cacti and succulents more susceptible. Prevention is better than cure, so make sure indoor and greenhouse plants are well ventilated and aren't sitting in moist soil. Nurturing beneficial microbes and fungi in the substrate can also protect against pathogens. Treat fungal diseases with sulphur-based fungicide sprays or sulphur powder. Cut away the affected area to stop it spreading, and dust the cut with sulphur powder. If the plant is covered in lesions, take cuttings of the unaffected parts, using a clean knife and dusting it with sulphur.

Fungal disease causes rust-coloured or black lesions on stems but can be treated with sulphur-based fungicides.

Etiolation

Symptoms Weak, thin, spindly, floppy growth.

Treatment When plants don't receive enough light their stems elongate, or etiolate, looking thin, weak, and sometimes floppy. This is irreversible. On a multi-stemmed plant, simply cut off the etiolated area. On a single-stemmed plant, unfortunately you will have to learn to love its new look. To avoid etiolation it's imperative to give the plant the right light intensity. Most need to be on a bright windowsill or very close to it. If the plant is stretching despite this position, you might want to consider supplementing with grow lights.

Cold or frost damage

Symptoms Brown blotches, brown translucent stem or leaves, an unusual smell, a mushy stem or leaves.

Treatment Most succulent plants are susceptible to frost damage. Sometimes this is superficial, but in severe cases a plant can die overnight. It's important to know plants' temperature limitations and to bring them indoors or provide adequate insulation outside during cold weather. Additionally, they should be kept totally dry to minimize the risk of freeze damage. Cut off the mushy parts and save what you can through propagation.

Corking

Symptoms The lower part of the stem hardens and turns light brown, like cork.

Treatment Lignification is the scientific term for plant tissue becoming woody with age – known as corking – and is nothing to worry about, but as red spider mites (see page 95) can cause damage that looks similar it's important to inspect the plant closely. As long as pests can't be seen and the stem doesn't feel soft or mushy, don't worry. Corking is a natural occurrence to help the plant's stability.

Leaning

Symptom The plant is leaning over or can't stand unsupported.

Treatment Leaning can be symptomatic of a plant trying to find more light. Rotate the pot a quarter-turn each time you water. If, however, it's not leaning in the direction of a light source, it could be that you simply have a species that doesn't naturally grow vertically. Research the species to clarify this.

Corking, when stems becomes tough and woody with age, is harmless but easily confused with red spider mite damage, so check the plant carefully.

Wrinkled or dried out

Symptoms Wrinkled leaves, leaf drop, or a shrunken stem.

Treatment Ridiculous as it may sound, cacti and succulents can suffer from lack of water. The solution would seem obvious, water it, but you must go slowly. Don't oversaturate the substrate, as it's likely some roots have died, so the plant might rot from sitting in a damp substrate. Wrinkling can also signify root rot (see page 90), so do check the roots. If all the roots have rotted, cut them off and propagate the stem (see page 74).

Sun stress and scorching

Symptoms Purple, red, or bleached leaves or stems. Light grey/brown scarring on one side of the plant.

Treatment It's a myth that all cacti and succulent plants like intense, direct sunlight. When moving plants from indoors to outside it's essential to acclimatize them so they don't burn. Put them in a semi-shaded area for the first week or two, then gradually introduce them to a sunnier spot. Some species prefer dappled or filtered sunlight, so always familiarize yourself with their native habitat before deciding where to locate them. If a plant shows signs of stress, move it to a different location or provide shading.

No flowers

Symptom Flower buds either don't form or they drop off.

Treatment If a plant doesn't receive enough light, it won't have the energy to flower. Move your plant to a location where it receives bright sunlight for at least six to eight hours a day. Most cacti prefer warm temperatures during the day and slightly cooler temperatures at night to induce flowering, and they are also sensitive to overwatering, which can lead to root rot, inhibiting flowers. Check the substrate is dry before watering, and add fertilizer during the growing season.

HOW TO GET A CHRISTMAS CACTUS TO FLOWER

Schlumbergera (see page 170) prefers to be close to a window that only receives direct sunlight for a few hours in the morning or late afternoon. Optimum conditions for flowering are approximately six weeks of short days (eight hours of daylight) and a slight drop in temperature from day to night may help. A period without water from around October to November is also suggested to help trigger flowering. High day or night temperatures (≥24°C/75°F) may cause the buds to abort.

For a truly floriferous *Schlumbergera*, avoid exposing it to continual high temperatures and too much direct sunlight.

Pests

We'd all rather pests stay away from our prized plant collection, but like it or not, they are part of a balanced ecosystem. So, instead of reaching for the nearest blow torch, channel your energy into identifying the pest and learning how to control them. Wherever possible, avoid using pesticides and harmful chemicals, as these can have a detrimental effect on the wider ecosystem. There are plenty of environmentally friendly options available.

Mealybugs (*Pseudococcidae* families)

Symptoms Deformed new growth, sticky sap, black mould, white cotton-wool-like specks, dried brown patches on the stem, or shrivelled leaves.

Identification Mealybugs are light pink, yellow, or light brown, but the powdery wax that covers their body is white. They have an oval or elongated body, resembling a woodlouse, with two long antennae. They suck the sap from leaves and stems, secreting a sticky honeydew that attracts mould spores, and often go unnoticed before the colony has grown into a problem. Check every plant you bring into your collection thoroughly. It's essential that populations aren't allowed to get out of hand, by which I mean more than two or three.

Treatment Use a small brush to directly dab the mealybugs with neat surgical spirit (rubbing alcohol). This works well on the ones you can see, but to ensure all mealybugs are killed, including the youngsters, fill a spray bottle with 75 per cent surgical spirit (rubbing alcohol) and 25 per cent water, then patch-test a small area to make sure it doesn't damage the plant, before spraying the whole plant.

For an infestation, diatomaceous earth (DE) can help. I recommend using food-grade

Mealybugs can appear as white cotton-wool-like patches (top). To treat, use a dry paintbrush to cover them with diatomaceous earth (above).

DE and wearing a mask when applying so as not to inhale dust particles. Using a dry brush, cover the whole plant with the powder, and make sure to keep it dry. Leave it on for as long as possible to kill the adults and hatchlings. After a week or so you can rinse the plant with water to remove the powder. Repeat if necessary.

Another option is to release beneficial insects onto the infested plant. Green lacewings (*Chrysoperla carnea*) are highly effective, and will also feed on aphids, thrips, and spider mites. The ladybird *Cryptolaemus montrouzieri* is also a prolific mealybug killer. If you decide to use this method, it is advisable to cover the plant (with a clear plastic bag or fine netting) so the predators don't escape and stay on the plant.

Visible mealybugs can be dabbed with neat methylated spirits, using a small paintbrush.

Red spider mites (*Tetranychus urticae*)

Symptoms Small brown dots where the plant's epidermis has been damaged. Brown patches and scarring. If left unnoticed the whole stem can be damaged and become a dull light brown. Fine webbing signifies a serious infestation.

Identification Despite their common name, these mites are a light yellowy-green colour with two black patches on their backs. In autumn, the females turn red prior to overwintering. They are minuscule, so a loupe or hand lens is advisable to identify them. Prolonged feeding on the plant's sap can cause permanent scarring, dehydration, and stunted growth, but the harm from viruses spread by the mites is a far greater concern, leading to severe damage or death. Plants may turn yellow or brown before dying.

Treatment Prevention is always better than cure so one of the best deterrents is to keep your plants clean. This removes dust (which spider mites like) and also helps the plant photosynthesize more efficiently, which makes it more resilient to pests. In winter, when I bring my plants indoors, I also give

A plant that has suffered severe red spider mite damage will look dull, brown, and scarred.

them a dusting of diatomaceous earth as a preventative measure (see the treatment for mealybugs, opposite).

Fill a spray bottle with 75 per cent surgical spirit (or rubbing alcohol) and 25 per cent water, then patch-test a small area. If your plant can tolerate the treatment, spray it thoroughly. Repeat every few days to ensure that the breeding cycle is broken.

Red spider mite can also be controlled by releasing their natural predator, *Phytoseiulus persimilis*, onto the plant.

False spider mites, flat mite, or red tea mite (*Tenuipalpidae* family)

Symptoms Mottling, scarring, brown and scabby discoloration, chlorosis, blistering, or bronzing.

Identification At a fraction of a millimetre in size, you will need a hand lens to help identify these. They are flat, oval, and dark green to browny-orange in colour. Unlike spider mites, false spider mites don't cause webbing. Ideal conditions for this species is 25–30°C (77–86°F) with high humidity. Small numbers can cause significant damage, which can be mistaken for corking (see page 92).

Treatment See red spider mites on page 95.

False spider mites, or flat mites, can cause unsightly brown and scabby patches on stems and leaves.

Root mealybugs (*Rhizoecus* species)

Symptoms Slow or stunted growth, a wilted appearance, and an overall decline in plant health.

Identification Check under the pot, around the drainage holes, or around the root ball for small, white, cottony masses. As the name suggests, root mealybugs feed on the roots and are a serious threat. They move slowly but purposefully between pots, prefer dry substrates, and can multiply rapidly during the winter dormancy period. Once the roots have been damaged, the plant is more susceptible to fungal diseases.

Treatment Knock off as much soil from the roots as possible and rinse them with water. Fill a small container with either 75 per cent water and 25 per cent horticultural soap, or 75 per cent surgical spirit (rubbing alcohol) and 25 per cent water, and soak the roots for an hour. Remove the plant and rinse the roots thoroughly. Set the plant aside and let the roots dry for 24 hours before repotting using fresh substrate.

Another option is to use predatory mites called *Stratiolaelaps scimitus*, which feed on fungus gnat larvae, thrips pupae, root aphids, and root mealybugs. They may also move up the plant foliage and feed on mealybugs above the soil. As a last resort, before tossing a plant out, you can cut off all the roots and treat it as a cutting (see propagation, page 74).

A mixture of horticultural soap and water can be an effective treatment for various pests.

Scale (*Coccoidea*)

Symptoms Areas where scale insects are feeding will turn brown.

Identification Mature scale insects look like tiny brown, waxy "scabs", which can be picked off with a fingernail. Younger nymphs may have an orange/yellow appearance. They feed on sap and excrete a sticky residue on the stems or leaves. Once feeding has begun, they coat themselves with a tough waxy secretion, which acts like a shell.

Treatment The waxy coating protects adults from contact insecticides, which are only effective against the nymph stage, known as "crawlers". Scale can, however, be controlled using horticultural soap, which suffocates them.

Cover the soil with a plastic bag so the scale insects don't fall onto it. Press strips of masking tape onto areas where you see scale, then peel them off, removing some of the insects with them. Repeat this process on all areas of the plant. Discard the used tape. Spray the plant with a 50:50 solution of water and surgical spirit (rubbing alcohol) or

Spray plants affected with scale insects or thrips with a mixture of either horticultural soap and water, or methylated spirits and water.

horticultural soap. Repeat the process if you see more appear. Alternatively, dust the entire plant with diatomaceous earth (DE), ensuring the powder stays dry.

Thrips (*Thysanoptera*)

Symptoms Leaves or stems have silvery patches. Injured plants are twisted, discoloured, and scarred. Tiny black dots of excrement can often be seen near the silvery patches.

Identification Thrips are slender winged insects, of which there are approximately 6,000 species. The bodies of adult thrips can be yellow, orange, red, brown, or black. Western flower thrips (*Frankliniella occidentalis*) particularly trouble cacti and succulents (especially *Lithops* and *Schlumbergera*, and others with large, flat cladodes). They feed on sap (and sometimes pollen), while the eggs are laid in leaves, stems, and flowers. The larvae can also be in the soil, making them difficult to control.

Treatment Spray the plant with a 50:50 solution of water and horticultural soap, which suffocates the adults. Wipe down the leaves and stem. Repeat every three to four days to break the life cycle.

There are several predatory mites that feed on thrips – *Stratiolaelaps scimitus* and *Amblyseius andersoni* both feed on the larvae, so can be good for keeping down the infestation. *Orius laevigatus* will feed on all stages of thrips – eggs, larvae, and adults.

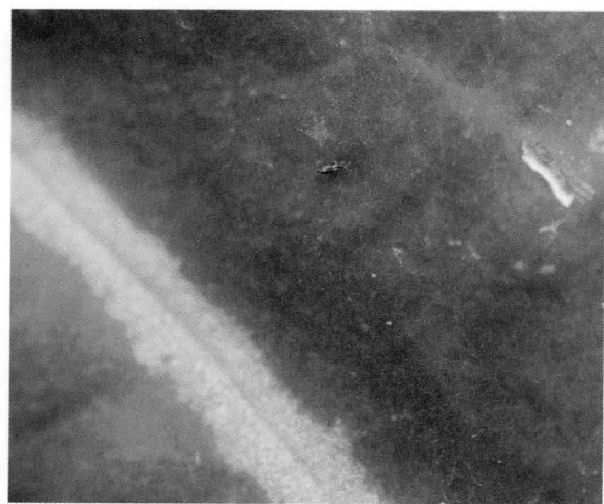

Sap-sucking thrips are tiny winged insects that particularly like cacti and succulents.

Damage from thrips appears as silvery patches on leaves and stems, and twisted, scarred leaves.

Vine weevil (*Otiorhynchus sulcatus*)

Symptoms The adult beetle is not the real problem. The larvae bore into the base of stems and feed on the roots, so the first sign can unfortunately be a collapsed, dead plant.

Identification Vine weevil larvae have a creamy-coloured body and brown head.

They are "C"-shaped, and approximately 10mm (½in) long. They feed on roots and rhizomes, which disrupts water and nutrient transport to above-ground plant tissues. The adults lay eggs on the surface of the soil in summer through to early autumn. Most plant losses occur during September to March, when the grubs are becoming fully grown.

Treatment The most natural way to control vine weevil is to encourage predators such as birds, frogs, toads, shrews, hedgehogs, and predatory ground beetles into your garden. Another environmentally friendly method is to use *Steinernema kraussei* nematodes – microscopic worms that kill the grubs. It can be difficult to ensure the conditions are entirely right to use a pathogenic nematode successfully, so always follow the instructions exactly.

Deformed leaves can be a sign of pest damage, so check your plants regularly.

Sciarid fly (also known as fungus gnats)

Symptoms Small flies, flying haphazardly near the plant and running around the soil.

Identification Easy-to-spot brown flies (or maggot-like larvae), which are mostly a problem indoors on houseplants. Although annoying, they won't cause much damage to mature plants but can cause problems for young plants, cuttings, and seedlings. The adults are attracted to moist soil, laying their eggs close to the base of the plant. The larvae mainly feed on organic matter but can also feed on the roots.

Treatment An infestation may indicate that you are watering your plants too frequently. Always check the soil to make sure it has dried out before watering and use a free-draining substrate. A two-pronged attack is necessary to tackle fungus gnats. Yellow sticky traps pushed into the soil will catch the adults, and beneficial nematodes (*Steinernema feltiae/carpocapsae*) watered into the soil will eat the larvae. (Note that nematodes need moist compost, so don't work in other growing substrates.) Fungus gnats feed on organic matter, so consider adding more grit or pumice to the potting mix to deter them.

What to Grow

Plant profiles introduction

In this section, we will explore a variety of cacti and succulents, which I've chosen for their distinctive characteristics and their suitability for growing at home, indoors or outside.

To help you choose plants that will thrive in your own environment, I've described their light requirements and, importantly, the temperatures they can tolerate. If you don't have outside space, I've included the requirements for growing the plants indoors, such as where to put them, what substrate to choose, and when to water them. Whether you are looking to create your own verdant oasis in your living room or make a statement in the garden, you will find an array of options to suit your needs in the myriad forms and colours these plants offer.

The plants have been divided into three subsections: Arid Habitat Cacti, Forest Habitat Cacti, and Succulents. This is because, contrary to popular belief, there are two distinct types of cacti: those that grow terrestrially in deserts, on rocky hillsides, and in scrublands, and those that grow in wetter, more humid forests, on trees or rocks. And although cacti are all succulent and belong to one family, other succulents belong to many families, so they need a section all their own. Due to the differences in their native habitats, all these plants not only look distinctive, but also have diverse care needs.

Plant names

Each plant has a unique standardized name and is classified into hierarchical categories based on its evolutionary relationships. An easy way to describe the main categories is this: one or more varieties make up a species; one or more species make up a genus; one or more genera (the plural of genus) make up a family. When scientists describe a new plant, they give it a "binomial" Latin name, which has two parts: first, the genus, then the species epithet (e.g. *Crassula ovata*). The genus name can be used by itself when talking about a group of succulents, but the species name is never used alone.

It doesn't end there, however. Other shorthand terms frequently appear in plant names to describe their many different forms. These include an "×" between two parent plant names to indicate a hybrid, "cv." for plants that come about through cultivation (rather than in the wild), "forma" or "f." for minor variations such as colour, "subsp." for subspecies, "var." to denote different variations of the common plant, and "synonym" or "syn." when a plant has been reclassified and renamed.

Most plants also have common names, which are far easier to remember and to say than most of the scientific names. Even these can lead to confusion, though, as one name can refer to an entirely different plant in another country. This is why the scientific names are vital, so it's universally understood what particular plant we are discussing. Unfortunately, succulent plants, particularly cacti, seem subject to frequent reclassification, which can be frustrating. While my aim in this book is to use the most current names, even by the time we go to print, some may well have changed.

Arid cacti are mostly terrestrial, found in areas that experience extreme drought and often extreme heat. Primarily thriving in deserts, but also in diverse landscapes including shrublands, mountains, and semi-arid grasslands, they have adapted to withstand intense sunlight, xeric soil, and being eaten by animals. Unlike forest cacti, they generally have ferocious spines, solid rather than flexible stems, and a higher tolerance to sunlight.

Arid Habitat Cacti

Ariocarpus

Family *Cactaceae*
Subfamily *Cactoideae*
Common name Living rock cactus, star cactus

There is something beautifully incongruous about an *Ariocarpus* in bloom when, in autumn, a delicate display of large cream or white flowers appears out of something resembling a rock.

This master of disguise lives in sandy, rocky areas of central and northern Mexico (except *Ariocarpus fissuratus*, which spreads into southern Texas). Like an iceberg, the plant's body is mostly hidden beneath the rocky terrain, with only the top granite-like tubercles protruding from beneath. As well as the beautiful blooms in autumn, a further softening of the harsh exterior is provided by fur-like trichomes, creating a fluffy wool that grows on top and in between the tubercles to help protect it from sun damage. Typically low-growing in a rosette formation, the triangular tubercles are flattened or protruding and, unlike most cacti, don't have spines, except as seedlings. Patience is required with these plants, as is writing them into your will – they are very slow-growing and can live for over a hundred years.

"A hard-as-nails rock star with an unexpectedly soft, fluffy centre"

Ariocarpus furfuraceus

Stone-like triangular tubercles blend in with the plant's rocky terrain

How to grow

Light

INDOORS Maximum light is essential to keep them happy – on the brightest windowsill or a conservatory is best.
OUTSIDE In an unshaded position in a greenhouse.

Temperature

Average minimum temperature of 5°C (41°F) is recommended for safety, although some species can tolerate lower than this provided they are kept bone dry.

Substrate

75% horticultural sand/grit, 25% potting compost.

Feeding

Once or twice during the growing season.

Water

Allow the soil to dry out completely between waterings. Keep dry if winter days are short and cold. Watering from the bottom will help keep the wool looking pristine and less like a matted sheep.

RECOMMENDED SPECIES

***Ariocarpus retusus* 'Scheidw.'**
One of the easiest and fastest growing (in a very slow way).

A. fissuratus
Plants have a rosette of brown or grey-green, wrinkled, triangular tubercles, resembling reptile skin.

Astrophytum

Family *Cactaceae*
Subfamily *Cactoideae*
Common name Star plant

The *Astrophytum* genus comprises a fascinating array of cacti, ranging from the sea urchin-like *Astrophytum asterias* to the peculiar *Astrophytum caput-medusae,* which resembles coral or an octopus with its long tubercles.

Astrophytum are from central, northern, and northwestern Mexico, where they can be found growing in different habitats: among rocks, in sand, and beneath bushes. The genus name is derived from the Greek, meaning "star plant". Typically, species are characterized by their globular or cylindrical shapes, distinctive ribs, and often minimal to no spines, so *Astrophytum* plants are easier to handle compared to other cacti. Some species within the genus showcase intriguing raised woolly spots or flecks, creating a striking contrast against their green or grey-green hues. Upon reaching maturity, typically between three and six years, they produce daisy-like yellow flowers from the crown.

"A flock of stars"

Astrophytum myriostigma* var. *quadricostatum

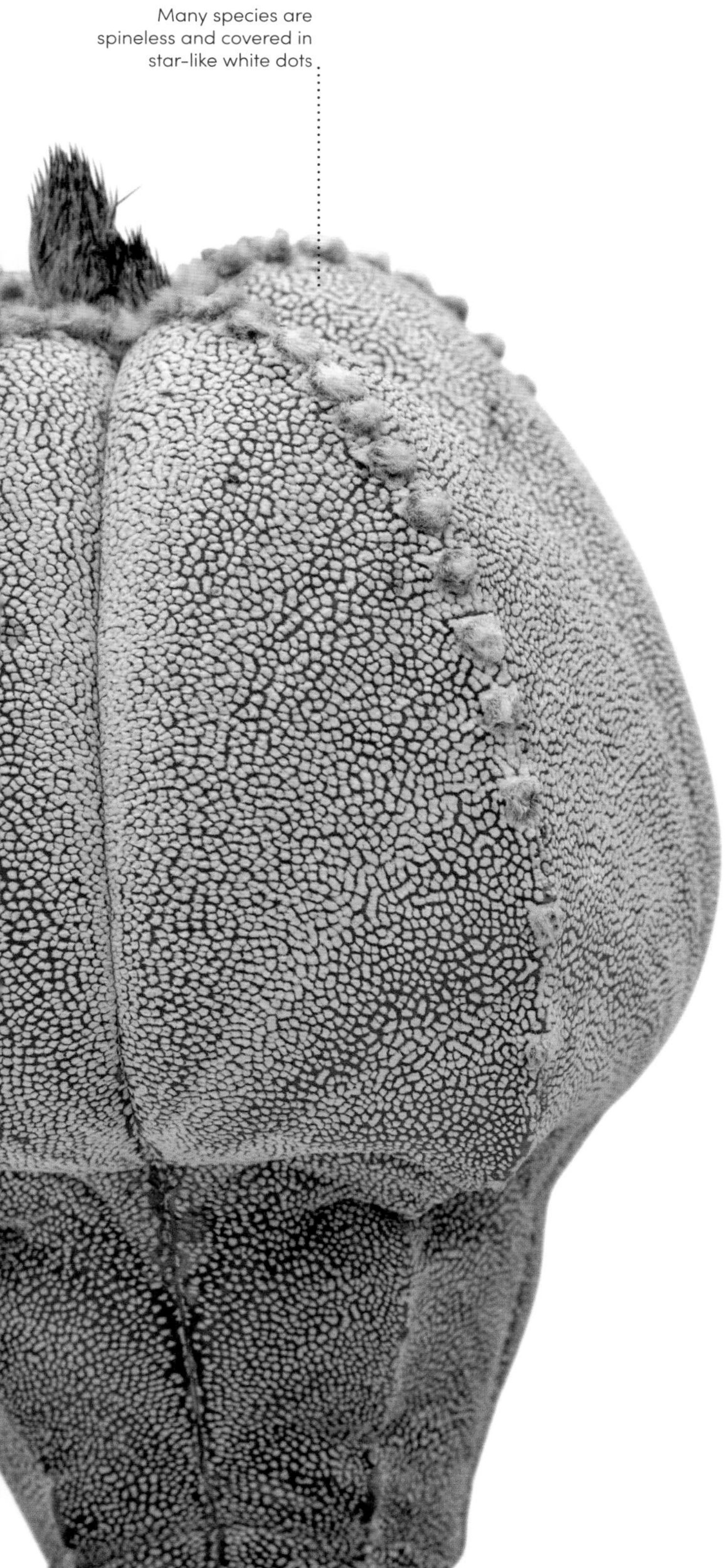

Many species are spineless and covered in star-like white dots

How to grow

Light

INDOORS The brightest south-facing windowsill or conservatory is necessary, with no shading needed at all from the sun.

OUTSIDE In full sun in a greenhouse. While it can be grown as a garden specimen in full sun, it is more commonly grown in a pot.

Temperature

Average minimum temperature of 5°C (41°F) is recommended for safety, although some species can tolerate lower than this provided they are kept bone dry.

Substrate

50% horticultural sand/grit, 50% potting compost.

Feeding

Once a month during the growing season.

Water

Allow soil to dry out completely between waterings. Keep dry if winter days are short and cold. Be careful not to overwater, especially *A. asterias*, which is easily killed this way.

RECOMMENDED SPECIES

Astrophytum myriostigma
Commonly known as bishop's cap, this spineless cactus with felty pads is one of the easiest to grow.

A. ornatum
Grows faster and larger than other species.

A. capricorne
Has long, curly, wire-like spines and glorious yellow flowers.

Blossfeldia

Family *Cactaceae*
Subfamily *Cactoideae*

Blossfeldia is a genus containing one – yes, ONE – species, and it holds the very special title of the smallest cactus in the world!

Blossfeldia liliputana is native to the high-altitude regions of Bolivia and Argentina, where their size rarely exceeds 12mm (½in) in diameter. Their colour and shape are similar to stones, lacking true spines and ribs; instead, they have a tiny button-like appearance. The diminutive size, however, does not deter the plant from producing disproportionately large white flowers.

Typically found growing between boulders on rocky slopes and often in crevices of rock faces, they can shrink during drought, losing up to 80 per cent of their water content, becoming almost flush with the rock surface, and rehydrate and swell when fog, mist, or rain returns. This remarkable ability to survive almost complete desiccation, and their tolerance of extreme temperatures and harsh sunlight, make this one very small but very tough cactus. They are highly sought-after by collectors as they are difficult to grow, so are often grafted onto another plant. They are also exceptionally slow-growing.

"Small but mighty"

Blossfeldia liliputana

How to grow

Light

INDOORS Position on a windowsill with direct sunlight or in a conservatory.
OUTSIDE Tolerant of full sun or semi-shade in a rocky area.

Temperature

Minimum temperature of no lower than 5°C (41°F), provided it's kept bone dry.

Substrate

25% potting compost, 75% horticultural grit/pumice.

Feeding

Once or twice during the growing season.

Water

Allow the soil to dry out completely between waterings. Keep dry if winter days are short and cold.

Tiny *Blossfeldia liliputana* produces wonderful outsized white flowers.

RECOMMENDED SPECIES

Blossfeldia liliputana
I can only recommend growing this one species as there are no others, although, unless you are confident in providing the right environment and have the skill required to care for it, I would recommend growing something easier. Having said that, many people have had success cultivating them from seed.

A solitary or clumping miniature cactus, with no ribs and no spines

Cephalocereus

Family *Cactaceae*
Subfamily *Cactoideae*
Common name Old man cactus

Cephalocereus are often characterized by their impressive height and distinctive spines, which vary from short to long and hairy, giving _C. senilis_ the common name old man cactus.

The hairy feature of *Cephalocereus* is not merely for show; it is a clever adaptation to protect the plant from the scorching sun during the day and the cold at night, and to collect moisture from the dew in its native habitat of southern Mexico. If the hair becomes too unruly, give it a brush or comb to neaten things up. Growing in a range of diverse landscapes from the seashore to mountainous slopes, these plants can reach up to 15 metres (49¼ft) and it's not unusual to see species that are hundreds of years old. *Cephalocereus* are night-blooming, unfurling often large white or pink, red, and yellow flowers that are as fleeting as they are beautiful. The blooms, which can take many years to produce, are specially adapted to attract nocturnal pollinators, such as moths and bats.

"Hair necessities"

Cephalocereus senilis

Cephalocereus can reach towering heights of up to 15 metres (49¼ft) in habitat

The hairy head of *Cephalocereus senilis* protects the plant from extremes of heat and cold.

RECOMMENDED SPECIES

Cephalocereus senilis
This is a small genus. The only species that is widely cultivated is *C. senilis*, which is no surprise given that it is by far the most unusual member of the family. I advise looking for a large, mature, second-hand specimen. The hairier the better.

How to grow

Light

INDOORS Bright, direct sunlight on a windowsill or in a conservatory is essential.
OUTSIDE This plant makes a great statement in a sunny, well-drained position in the garden. It needs protection from rain and frost at low temperatures.

Temperature

Average minimum temperature of 5–10°C (41–50°F) although some species can tolerate lower than this provided they are kept bone dry.

Substrate

50% potting compost, 50% horticultural sand/grit.

Feeding

Once a month during the growing season.

Water

Allow the soil to dry out completely between waterings. Keep dry if winter days are short and cold.

Cereus

Family *Cactaceae*
Subfamily *Cactoideae*
Common name Peruvian apple cactus, Andes organ pipe, giant club cactus, hedge cactus

Derived from the Latin word meaning "wax", "torch", or "candle", *Cereus* is one of the oldest names in the *Cactaceae* family, dating back to 1625. It perfectly describes this often-towering columnar cactus, topped with luminous white flowers that bloom at night.

Native to South America, *Cereus* is a varied genus comprising branching and shrubby species, as well as very large columnar specimens that can reach 25 metres (82ft) in height in the case of *Cereus stenogonus*. The majority of columnar cacti (over 500 species) from the seventeenth century onwards were given the name *cereus*. Over the centuries, through reclassification, there are currently 34 accepted species in the genus, although many other genera still include the suffix "*-cereus*", for example *Hylocereus*, *Pachycereus*, *Cephalocereus*, *Selenicereus*, and *Stenocereus*.

Many have large, white, showy, scented flowers, which open at night to attract pollinators, such as moths and bats. The fruits of *Cereus repandus* (or syn. *C. peruvianus*, depending on which you prefer), commonly known as Peruvian apple, are tasty, and if grown outside, the plants are very productive, yielding multiple crops per year.

"Waxing lyrical"

Cereus has defined ribs with a thick, waxy cuticle

Cereus hildmannianus

How to grow

Light

INDOORS Bright, direct sunlight on a windowsill or in a conservatory is essential.
OUTSIDE Full sun in a greenhouse or garden.

Temperature

Average minimum temperature of 5°C (41°F) is recommended for safety, although some species can tolerate lower than this for a very short period provided they are kept bone dry and it warms up during the day.

Substrate

50% potting compost, 50% horticultural sand/grit/perlite.

Feeding

Once a month during the growing season.

Water

Must be allowed to fully dry out before watering. Keep dry in cold temperatures.

The spiralling growth habit of *Cereus forbesii spiralis* is believed to derive from a mutation spotted in the wild and cloned for cultivation.

RECOMMENDED SPECIES

Cereus aethiops
A shrubby, sometimes prostrate cactus with black spines. Will flower when young.

C. forbesii spiralis
A species with a striking corkscrew growth habit.

***C. jamacaru* and *C. repandus* (syn. *peruvianus*)**
Grow these outside and enjoy the delicious fruit.

Cleistocactus

Family *Cactaceae*
Subfamily *Cactoideae*
Common name Silver torch, woolly torch, golden rat tail cactus

Cleistocactus are characterized by dense white or yellow spines, making some appear fluffy, but they are in no way soft and cuddly; stroke them at your peril.

Native to mountainous areas, the *Cleistocactus* genus is spread throughout Peru, Uruguay, Bolivia, and Argentina, growing in large, upright, shrubby clumps, or hanging or creeping along the ground and over boulders. The flowers resemble a lipstick in shape and colour, or unexploded fireworks, and are seldom fully open; hence the name *kleistos,* meaning "closed" in Greek. They also look pretty funny, sticking out horizontally on some of the upright species.

"Hardy with a soft exterior"

A dense covering of "hair" protects stems from cold and heat

Cleistocactus strausii

Cleistocactus winteri, commonly known as golden rat tail.

How to grow

Light

INDOORS Close to a bright window, or they will do well in a conservatory.

OUTSIDE They make a great statement plant in a sunny, well-drained position in the garden, in a pot, or in a porch.

Temperature

Most are frost hardy if kept dry but it's best to cover them in fleece and protect them from temperatures 0°C (32°F) and below.

Substrate

50% horticultural sand/grit, 50% potting compost.

Feeding

Once a month during the growing season.

Water

Allow to fully dry out before watering again.

RECOMMENDED SPECIES

Cleistocactus strausii

If I could only choose one plant to keep from my entire collection, it would be my lovely old *Cleistocactus strausii.* Very easy to care for and tolerant of low temperatures. Mine lives in an unheated greenhouse where temperatures, on rare occasions, can reach as low as -9°C (16°F).

C. winteri

Commonly known as the golden rat tail cactus because of the yellow spines, which create a golden hue and almost obscure the stem beneath. It looks spectacular in a hanging pot or basket in front of a window, or in a conservatory or porch.

C. brookei

Sports golden spines on erect or sprawling stems.

Copiapoa

Family *Cactaceae*
Subfamily *Cactoideae*

A survivor in extremely arid conditions, this cactus is a tough (but sometimes tiny) and relatively unfussy plant that comes in an unusual array of colours.

The genus *Copiapoa* takes its name from the town of Copiapoa in northern Chile, where it is rife in the Atacama Desert. Some species are tiny, solitary plants measuring only a few centimetres or inches across, while others exceed 1 metre (3¼ft) in height or form imposing mounds with hundreds of stems. Their colour sets them apart from many other cacti, with species ranging from a floury white through grey-green to dark brown and almost black. Most species produce tubular yellow flowers, which grow from woolly crowns on the apex in summer.

Despite the Atacama Desert being one of the driest places on Earth, where annual rainfall is barely 1mm (0.03in), *Copiapoa* thrive by harvesting moisture from "*la Camanchaca*", marine stratocumulus cloud banks that form on the Chilean coast. Despite their extreme and specific conditions in habitat, *Copiapoa* aren't difficult to cultivate. On the whole the genus is forgiving and will flower from a young age, though most species are very slow-growing.

"Tough but forgiving"

Copiapoa haseltoniana

How to grow

Light

INDOORS The brightest windowsill or conservatory.
OUTSIDE In full sun or partial shade. In a greenhouse, they must be in a position with good air circulation to prevent sunburn.

Temperature

Average minimum temperature of 5°C (41°F) is recommended for safety, although some species can tolerate lower than this for a very short period provided they are kept bone dry and it warms up during the day.

Substrate

25% potting compost, 75% horticultural sand/grit/perlite.

Feeding

Once a month during the growing season.

Water

Allow the soil to dry out completely between waterings. Avoid watering from July to August when some will go dormant. Keep dry if winter days are short and cold.

Mist condenses on spines and stems, then trickles down to the roots

RECOMMENDED SPECIES

Copiapoa cinerea
Has a white, waxy stem, which contrasts beautifully with the black spines. Needs good light to develop the white colour.

C. hypogaea
Forms a cluster of squat, round stems, which are dark green to brown in colour.

C. humilis
A small, easy-growing species that is sometimes solitary but usually clumping at the base.

Grower profile

Graham Charles

Location Rutland, UK

Membership President of the British Cactus and Succulent Society

Graham owns one of the largest and most impressive private collections of cacti and succulents in the UK. A grower for over 60 years, he has written numerous books, including his latest on the genus *Gymnocalycium*.

How many plants do you have in your collection?

Every year I grow hundreds of plants from seed, so my collection has large numbers of young plants. I probably have more than 5,000 plants in all.

Which plant(s) are you most proud of?

I have been fortunate to be able to see cacti in their habitats on many occasions. During our trips to South America, my friends and I have discovered previously unknown cacti, which we have subsequently published as new species. I am proud of this legacy and the seedlings I am growing of these new plants with the aim of producing seeds and establishing them in cultivation.

What's been your biggest failure, and what did you learn from that experience?

There is a great temptation to accumulate more and more plants, eventually creating such a burden of maintenance that it is

Graham Charles with some of his plants, including several that are growing in the ground.

impossible to keep all the plants healthy – when a hobby becomes such chore it ceases to be a pleasure. I got there but have now accepted that I cannot grow everything and am concentrating on South American species – my favourites.

Where would you recommend seeing cacti in their native habitat?

The best place to start is southwest USA (Texas, Arizona, California, etc.). I like South America most and would recommend Chile as a particularly pleasant country to visit. Argentina and Peru are also dramatic, and Brazil has a remarkable cactus flora, so long as you get help to find it!

Is there a common myth about growing cacti or succulents that you'd like to debunk?

I volunteer at a garden centre where cacti and succulents are for sale. I hear visitors talking about the plants and misconceptions are plentiful. It is common to hear that the plants don't need to be watered. I think this is the myth I would most like to correct.

What advice would you give beginners?

I would say grow the plants that take your fancy. Don't be afraid to make mistakes. Avoid rare or difficult plants until you are more experienced so you aren't discouraged. Choose the brightest location for your plants, such as a south- or west-facing windowsill, conservatory, or glasshouse.

Five plants everyone should grow?

1. ***Mammillaria hahniana.*** A beautiful, symmetrical cactus from Mexico. The best forms are covered in hairs, and in spring it produces a ring of pretty pink flowers.

2. ***Aylostera muscula.*** Densely covered in white spines, this small cactus from Bolivia puts on a show of orange flowers in spring. There are also many hybrids of this species, which have the benefit of a long flowering period.

Aloe variegata, an easy-to-grow favourite, flowering in spring.

3. ***Haworthia truncata.*** A South African succulent. This plant has curious truncated leaves with "windows" in their ends. It soon makes clumps of stems, which produce small flowers on long stalks.

4. ***Aloe variegata.*** A classic favourite with nicely marked leaves arranged in a triangle. Long flower stalks produce typical *Aloe* flowers, pollinated by birds in its native South African home.

5. ***Agave victoria-reginae.*** With its dramatic rosette of beautifully marked leaves, this small, slow-growing Mexican *Agave* makes a spectacular plant. It will take decades to grow large enough to flower, when it produces a spectacular, tall inflorescence, after which the plant dies.

Echinocereus

Family *Cactaceae*
Subfamily *Cactoideae*
Common name Hedgehog cactus, kingcup cactus

***Echinocereus* owe their popularity to their dramatic spines and possibly the most stunning flowers of the *Cactaceae* family. The spines display hues of white, yellow, red, and even purple, sometimes in dense clusters that create a striking starburst.**

Echinocereus comprises about 70 species native to the southern US and Mexico, where they grow in a wide variety of habitats, including coastal plains, rocky mountain slopes, desert scrub, and in the understories of ponderosa pine-oak woodlands. Many species feature large, brightly coloured blooms, but the most spectacular are the two-toned flowers with different-coloured inner and outer petals, which look almost unreal. Another distinctive characteristic of the genus is their "erumpent flowers". This refers to the way the flower buds develop internally before bursting through the epidermis of the stem, thought to be an adaptation to protect the buds from cold temperatures.

Most species are small, rarely taller than 46cm (18in), although they can form large mounds or clusters of stems. Plants exhibit varying degrees of spination, some ferocious-looking, while others are small, colourful, and give the stem a pinkish appearance. *Echinocereus* make great potted plants as they are compact and easy to care for, and when they bloom you will need to take time off work simply to sit and stare.

"Bursting with flowers"

Some species have long, ferocious multicoloured spines.

How to grow

Light

INDOORS On the brightest windowsill or in a conservatory.
OUTSIDE Direct sunlight.

Temperature

Many species are cold hardy if kept dry. Some, such as *E. triglochidiatus*, can tolerate –15°C (5°F). If in doubt keep above minimum 5°C (41°F).

Substrate

50% potting compost,
50% horticultural sand/grit.

Feeding

Once a month during the growing season.

Water

Allow the substrate to completely dry out between waterings. If you experience cold winters, don't water at all during this season unless the leaves are shrivelling.

***Echinocereus triglochidiatus* var. *gonacanthus* is also known as the claret cup cactus for its flowers.**

RECOMMENDED SPECIES

Echinocereus rigidissimus* var. *rubispinus

Produces coloured horizontal bands of spines around the stem with large, showy, vibrant magenta flowers.

E. reichenbachii

Also known as lace cactus. It has a small, cylindrical habit with white spines and a stunning fuchsia-pink flower with a darker purple-red centre. One of the hardier species.

E. knippelianus

Has globular bluish-green coloured stems and very thin yellow spines, making it look almost devoid of spines. In spring it has lovely funnel-shaped pink or white flowers.

Echinocereus fasciculatus

Echinopsis

Family *Cactaceae*
Subfamily *Cactoideae*
Common name Peanut cactus, sea-urchin cactus, hedgehog cactus, Easter lily cactus

With names such as hedgehog, sea-urchin, and peanut, you might be forgiven for thinking this genus comprises only small, cute plants, but as the genus grows so does the size of the species, which also (currently) includes large columnar plants.

Echinopsis species are native to Argentina, Bolivia, Peru, Brazil, Paraguay, and Uruguay, growing in many different locations, including some at high altitude. The genus is in what seems like constant flux, with species from other genera, such as *Acanthocalycium, Cleistocactus,* and *Trichocereus,* being periodically included. As a result, *Echinopsis* comprises small, flattened-globose plants and large, tree-like giants with a long list of synonyms for many of the species.

One of the most remarkable features of *Echinopsis* plants are the beautiful, fragrant, trumpet-like flowers, which open only at night to be pollinated by moths. The flowers can be many times larger than the body of small species. Each flower only lasts a day or two but is quite the reward for proper care in cultivation. Small species are good for indoor growing, while the larger columnar species make exceptional landscape plants in warm regions.

"Blowing their own trumpet"

Echinopsis flowers are spectacular and fragrant but only open at night.

How to grow

Light

INDOORS Bright, direct sunlight on a windowsill or in a conservatory.
OUTSIDE Full sun in a greenhouse or garden.

Temperature

Average minimum temperature of 5°C (41°F) is recommended for safety, although some species can tolerate lower than this provided they are kept bone dry.

Substrate

50% potting compost, 50% horticultural sand/grit/perlite.

Feeding

Once a month during the growing season.

Water

Must be allowed to fully dry out before watering. Keep dry in cold temperatures.

RECOMMENDED SPECIES

Echinopsis oxygona
A classic, easy-to-grow cactus that is great as a houseplant. The flowers are large, showy, and scented.

E. eyriesii
Probably the best known and one of the most commonly grown *Echinopsis*. It is widely grown for the huge nocturnal flowers.

E. arachnacantha
Has recurved spines, which resemble small spiders. Large yellow, orange, or occasionally white or red flowers appear in early summer.

E. chamaecereus
A popular houseplant, known as the peanut cactus. Stems grow upright and cascade as they lengthen. Beautiful red flowers.

Some *Echinopsis* species have very long, fierce spines

Others can be almost spineless, or with very short cream spines

***Echinopsis chiloensis* var. *borealis* (left); *Echinopsis subdenudata* (right)**

Ferocactus

Family *Cactaceae*
Subfamily *Cactoideae*
Common name Barrel cactus

The name *Ferocactus* derives from the Latin word *ferox,* meaning "fierce". If you've ever brushed against one, you'll know why.

Native to the southwestern United States, many parts of Mexico, and islands in the Gulf of California, *Ferocactus* plants are usually barrel-shaped, characterized by strong, vicious spines, although some are clump-forming or rounded. Some species can reach about 3 metres (10ft) high and 60cm (24in) in diameter. They are slow to flower but the beautiful, often colourful spines are fast-growing to make up for it. Spines come in a wide range of colours; yellow, grey, white, brown, pinkish, or brilliant red – I advise buying one with the latter, often known as fire barrel, as the spines are the colour of fire.

When the plant does eventually bloom, the bell-shaped flowers often form a cluster or ring around the apex and are usually yellow, orange, purplish, or red. The fruits are also a feature, bearing an uncanny resemblance to little pineapples. *Ferocactus* have a very shallow root system and are therefore easily dislodged in heavy floods. The spines not only protect the plant when it's on the move, but actively help it to spread throughout the landscape, by attaching themselves to unsuspecting animals who may carry them to more favourable locations.

"Fiery, formidable, and ferociously beautiful"

How to grow

Light

INDOORS Direct sunlight on the brightest windowsill or in a conservatory.

OUTSIDE Full sun.

Temperature

If kept completely dry, some species can withstand temperatures below freezing, but for safety it's best to maintain a minimum temperature of 5°C (41°F).

Substrate

50% potting compost, 50% horticultural sand/grit/perlite.

Feeding

Once a month during the growing season.

Water

Allow the soil to dry out completely between waterings. Keep dry if winter days are short and cold.

RECOMMENDED SPECIES

Ferocactus latispinus
Has striking red or white flattened, curved spines.

F. pilosus
Also known as Mexican fire barrel, this is one of the most striking owing to its size – it can grow up to 3 metres (10ft) in habitat – and its bright yellow or red spines.

F. chrysacanthus
Armed with long, curved, yellow spines that become grey as the plant matures. Very slow-growing.

The barrel-shaped stem erupts with fierce, colourful spines

Ferocactus latispinus

Gymnocalycium

Family *Cactaceae*
Subfamily *Cactoideae*
Common name Chin cactus

An easy-to-grow plant that will tolerate relatively low light levels, this cactus is perfect for beginners as well as more advanced growers and will flower with little effort.

Gymnocalycium is a genus of about 70 species found throughout Argentina, parts of Uruguay, Paraguay, southern Bolivia, and parts of south Brazil. Some species have a protuberance below each spine-bearing areole, which some think looks like a chin, hence the common name. They are characterized by their spherical stem and smooth flowers (without any spines, wool, or bristles), which emerge from the top of the cactus in shades of white, red, pink, or green. A well-grown plant will often flower several times during the year.

Some species grow in dry forests in dappled shade and therefore tolerate lower light levels than many other cacti, which makes them well suited to indoor growing. *Gymnocalycium mihanovichii* has become a popular species due to its mutant cultivars, which lack chlorophyll, exposing the red, orange, or yellow pigmentation. You will often see these cultivars grafted onto *Hylocereus* and sold as a "moon cactus". Be warned, though: even with good care these mutants are relatively short-lived.

"Easy-going and free-flowering"

Gymnocalycium mihanovichii

How to grow

Light

INDOORS Bright, direct light on a windowsill or in a conservatory is preferable for many species, but they will tolerate lower light than most other cacti.

OUTSIDE Shade from the midday sun in a greenhouse. Dappled sunlight in the garden.

Temperature

Average minimum temperature of 5°C (41°F) is recommended for safety, although some species can tolerate lower than this provided they are kept bone dry.

Substrate

50% potting compost, 50% horticultural sand/grit.

Feeding

Once a month during the growing season.

Water

Allow the soil to dry out completely between waterings. Keep dry if winter days are short and cold.

RECOMMENDED SPECIES

Gymnocalycium denudatum
Has a dark-green body with contrasting light, recurved spines that resemble spiders.

G. saglionis
The giant chin cactus is the largest species, reaching up to 30cm (1ft) wide in habitat. It has long, thick recurved spines and pink or flesh-coloured flowers.

G. bruchii
Forms clumps of blue-green stems with woolly areoles and white-grey spines. One of the most cold-tolerant South American species.

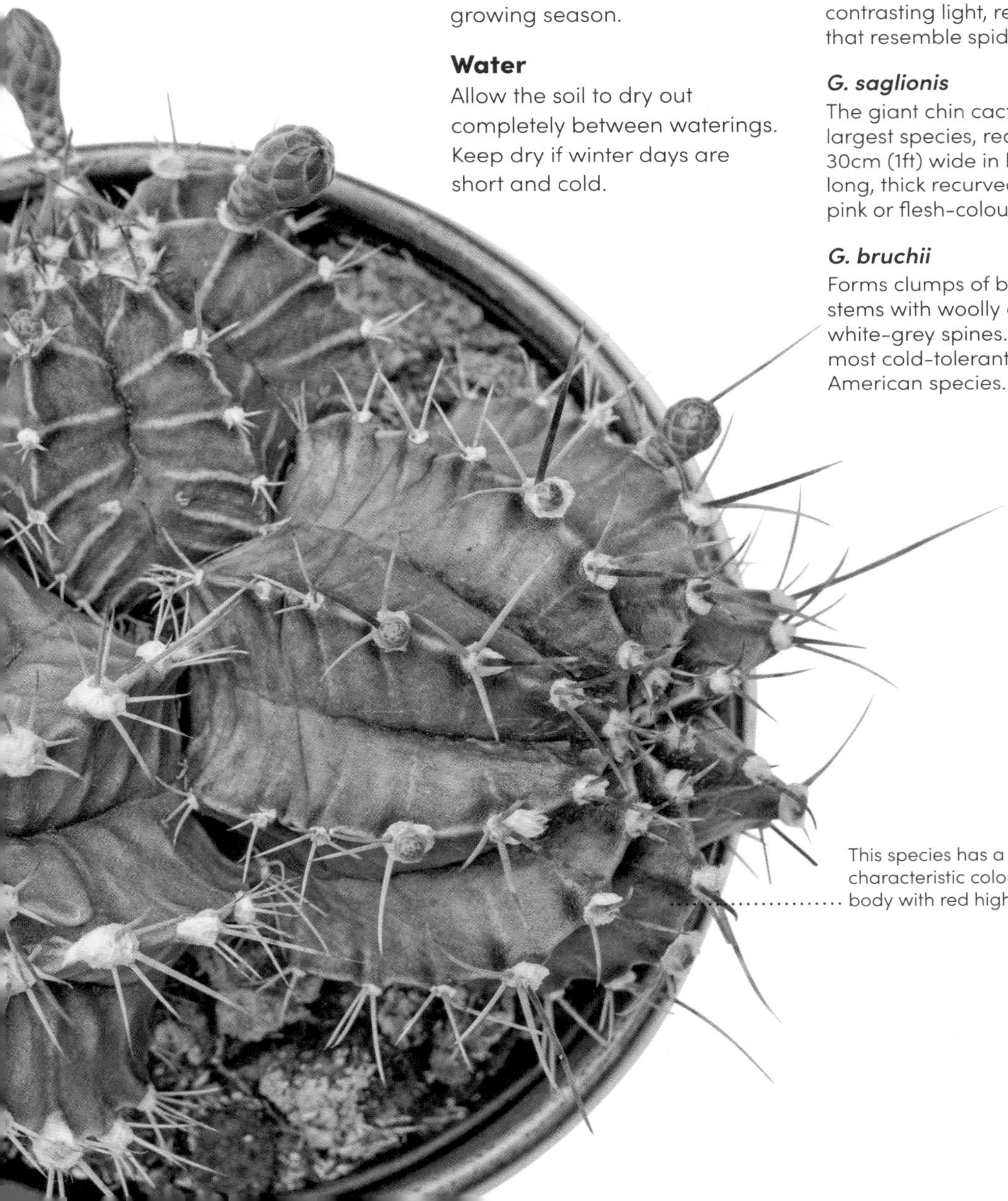

This species has a characteristic colourful body with red highlights

Mammillaria

Family *Cactaceae*
Subfamily *Cactoideae*
Common name Birthday cake cactus, pincushion cactus, nipple cactus, thumb cactus

---

The reddish-brown spines of this species are hooked

Mammillaria bombycina

"The sleeping beauty of the cactus world"

Rather like humans, some members of this family become lazy with age and prefer to be recumbent. Give them a bed to lie in and they will grow happily for years.

Containing approximately 200 species, *Mammillaria* are one of the largest and most popular genera of cacti. Most species are endemic to Mexico where the globose or columnar plants grow either in a solitary fashion or in clumps forming massive mounds. The name derives from the Latin word *mammilla* meaning "nipple" or "teat", owing to the shape of the conical or rounded tubercles, in between which the flowers grow. In some species the flowers are small and pink, forming a crown around the top of the stem, while others are yellow or white. A few species have larger, showier flowers, which protrude further above the plant. If you have a healthy *Mammillaria*, with no signs of rotting at the base, which is struggling to stand upright, it might be more comfortable lying down and growing horizontally. I use a long, rectangular terracotta pot as a bed for my 40-year-old *M. spinosissima* subsp. *pilcayensis*.

Some species, like this *Mammillaria spinosissima*, lack the internal backbone of a columnar cactus so will, in time, grow horizontally.

How to grow

Light

INDOORS Bright, direct light on a windowsill or in a conservatory.
OUTSIDE In an unshaded position in a greenhouse. Also makes a great feature plant in full sun among large rocks in the garden. If you live in a colder region, it is best to grow these cacti in pots so they can be brought indoors.

Temperature

Average minimum temperature of 5°C (41°F) is recommended for safety, although some species can tolerate lower than this provided they are kept bone dry.

Substrate

50% horticultural sand/grit, 50% potting compost.

Feeding

Once a month during the growing season.

Water

Allow the soil to dry out completely between waterings. Keep dry if winter days are short and cold.

RECOMMENDED SPECIES

Mammillaria matudae
Grows stems from the base to form a cluster and reclines as it elongates. Each stem has a ring of small magenta flowers.

M. spinosissima* subsp. *pilcayensis
A great starter plant for newbie cactus growers.

Melocactus

Family *Cactaceae*
Subfamily *Cactoideae*
Common name Pope's head, melon cactus

There is nothing comparable to *Melocactus* in the *Cactaceae* family – and when you've seen one with its top hat on you won't ever mistake it for anything else!

This genus currently contains approximately 40 species, native to the Caribbean, western Mexico, Central America, and northern South America, and it is fascinating in appearance. While a young plant will look much the same as any other globose cactus, when they reach maturity they begin to develop a cephalium, which is a dense mass of areoles with bristles that form a crazy-looking yellow, orange, red, or white "cap" directly on top of the stem. After the cephalium forms, the stem stops growing but the "cap" carries on and can reach over 1 metre (3¼ft) in height. The purpose of it is reproduction. It's from this structure that flowers appear, which are pink, magenta, or red, and produce edible fruits resembling tiny peppers that are nestled within the woolly cephalium. It is very satisfying to remove them for propagation!

"The mad hatter"

Melocactus matanzanus

How to grow

Light

INDOORS Direct sunlight on the brightest, warmest windowsill or in a conservatory that doesn't get too cold in winter.
OUTSIDE Likes full sun but will benefit from light shading in very high temperatures.

Temperature

Best kept above 10°C (50°F) as they are very sensitive to cold temperatures.

Substrate

25% potting compost,
75% horticultural sand/grit/perlite/pumice.

Feeding

Once a month during the growing season.

Water

Allow the soil to dry out completely between waterings. Keep dry if winter days are short and cold.

The hat-like cephalium forms atop the stem and can reach a great height

The cephalium is made of tightly packed axillary buds, short spines, and trichomes.

RECOMMENDED SPECIES

Melocactus azureus
Attractive icy-blue-green cactus hailing from a small area in Brazil called Bahia. When it reaches maturity, a whitish spherical cephalium develops, from which small magenta flowers bloom between spring and autumn.

M. intortus
The stem can reach 1 metre (3¼ft) high, making it the largest species of the genus. The spines are a browny-red and the flowers pink.

M. neryi
One of the easier *Melocactus* species to grow.

Myrtillocactus

Family *Cactaceae*
Subfamily *Cactoideae*
Common name Candelabra cactus, blue candle, boobie cactus, blue myrtle cactus

This branch-forming cactus can grow extraordinarily tall, and usually resembles a candelabra, though one particularly popular cultivar has a rather more unusual look.

Myrtillocactus is a small genus of five currently accepted species, the best known being *M. geometrizans*, or the blue myrtle cactus. Most of the five species will reach impressive heights, the average being 3–5 metres (10–16½ft), with *M. schenckii* potentially reaching a massive 7 metres (23ft). Generally, the stems of these plants are elongated, with a prolific branching growth pattern that starts lower down on the main trunk, resulting in a chandelier-type appearance in more mature plants. Young plants in cultivation often remain as one unbranched stem for many years.

The stems have around five to six ridges, along which the areoles are evenly spaced. Spines vary between species and cultivars, with some almost entirely absent and others long, hard, and sharp. The white or greenish-white flowers appear in summer, after which edible blue berries grow, called garambullos.

"Great heights, unusual forms"

Abnormal growth causes plants to fan out into a wavy, crest-like shape

Myrtillocactus geometrizans* f. *cristata

How to grow

Light

INDOORS Direct sunlight on the brightest windowsill or in a conservatory.
OUTSIDE Full sun.

Temperature

Average minimum temperature of 10°C (50°F) is recommended for safety, although some species can tolerate lower than this for a very short period, provided they are kept bone dry and it warms up during the day.

Substrate

50% potting compost, 50% horticultural sand/grit/perlite.

Feeding

Once a month during the growing season.

Water

Allow the soil to dry out completely between waterings. Keep dry if winter days are short and cold.

RECOMMENDED SPECIES

Myrtillocactus geometrizans* cv. *fukurokuryuzinboku
A Japanese cultivar that has become a sought-after novelty, due to its unusual protrusions, earning it the name boobie cactus. Who wouldn't want one?

M. geometrizans* f. *cristata
An awe-inspiring, contorted blue cactus that produces almost cloud-shaped growth. Worth the price tag.

Grower profile

Edgar Vargas

(@yourcactisuccs)

Location Bellflower, California

Specialism Cactus and succulent propagation

After working for many years in a plant nursery, Edgar started growing his own collection. He now propagates and sells cacti and succulents.

When did you first become interested in cacti and succulents?

My father opened his wholesale nursery after emigrating from Jalisco, Mexico, in 1997. I was only three years old. I would work at the nursery on weekends and any school breaks, which gave me a broad understanding of the plant world at an early age. When the COVID-19 pandemic hit I started to get a liking for collecting plants. That's when the cactus and succulent world came into my life. I've been collecting, propagating, and selling for about four years now.

How many plants do you have in your collection?

At this moment I have 219 plants in my collection, but I care for thousands in my greenhouse.

If you could only keep three plants from your collection, which would they be?

1. *Dorstenia gigas* f. *bullata*. A plant from the island of Socotra. Sheep grazing has decimated the population in nature. I'd like to propagate and eventually make them available for collectors worldwide.

2. *Eriosyce aurata.* Abarrel cactus from Chile. It has the most beautiful spines and rich green colour I've ever seen.

3. *Euphorbia clavigera.* A 30-plus-year-old plant that I rescued from a collector who was moving away. It's a caudex plant that stores a lot of energy in the big tubercle roots.

How do you deal with pests?

I believe in the right amount of airflow and lighting. This will do wonders. I also use 28g (1oz) of dish soap and 29ml (1fl oz) of mouthwash in a spray bottle, well shaken. I usually pick the bugs off as best I can, then spray on a cool day or in the late afternoon. It seems to work for a minor infestation.

An assortment of *Astrophytum asterias* with different-coloured blooms.

Is there a common myth about growing cacti or succulents that you'd like to debunk?

A common myth I hear is to only water your cactus a little bit. Actually, we need to completely soak the substrate. It's just that the watering cycles are a lot more spread apart than your typical leafy plant.

What advice would you give beginners?

Do not water after repotting! Make sure to acclimatize your cactus to its new environment slowly. Gradually introduce sun exposure until the skin can resist it all day, to avoid burns and scars.

Five plants everyone should grow?

1. *Dorstenia* is overlooked and unique in its growth habits and flower structures.
2. *Turbinicarpus* species are small, mostly clumping cacti that grow extremely slowly but are perfect for collectors who only have limited space.
3. *Dioscorea elephantipes.* A caudex plant in the yam family that creates a corky round trunk and a delicate vine in the cooler months.
4. *Alluaudia montagnacii.* Everyone has the Madagascar ocotillo, but if you're looking for a more viscous, metal-looking plant, this one's for you.
5. *Copiapoa.* One of the most popular genera at the moment. Super-cool cacti!

What are your top tips for plant care?

Research the plant species and where they come from. Every plant has its requirements. The more you can mimic the conditions of where it's from, the better off you will be. Also, be aware of your conditions and your growing zone (see page 52). What works for me in California may not work for other parts of the world.

Dorstenia gigas f. *bullata*, a plant prized by many collectors, from the island of Socotra, Yemen.

Opuntia

Family *Cactaceae*
Subfamily *Opuntioideae*
Common name Prickly pear

When you picture a classic desert cactus, it is probably *Opuntia,* or prickly pear, that you're thinking of. It might be well known, but this diverse genus has plenty of surprises in store.

Opuntia are the quintessential paddle-shaped, flattened cacti that we are all familiar with, though the genus includes diverse shapes and sizes, from tall, slender columns to shrub-like plants. The spination also varies greatly between species, with some having little more than tiny velvety-looking glochids on each areole, while others have clusters of long, vicious spines. The flowers of most species are large, showy, and relatively short-lived. However, after the flowers wither, several species produce edible fruit, known as prickly pears, which taste like a cross between melon, kiwi, and bubblegum. The pads, known as "nopales", are also used in numerous recipes throughout Mexico.

Many species of *Opuntia* are cold hardy, making them good candidates for outdoor planting in cooler climates. (Note, however, that *O. ficus-indica* is considered highly invasive in some countries.) The species of this large genus are easily hybridized, which can make identification challenging but has also enabled growers to develop cultivars suited to specific applications, whether that be ornamental use, landscaping, or fruit production.

"Familiar and fruity"

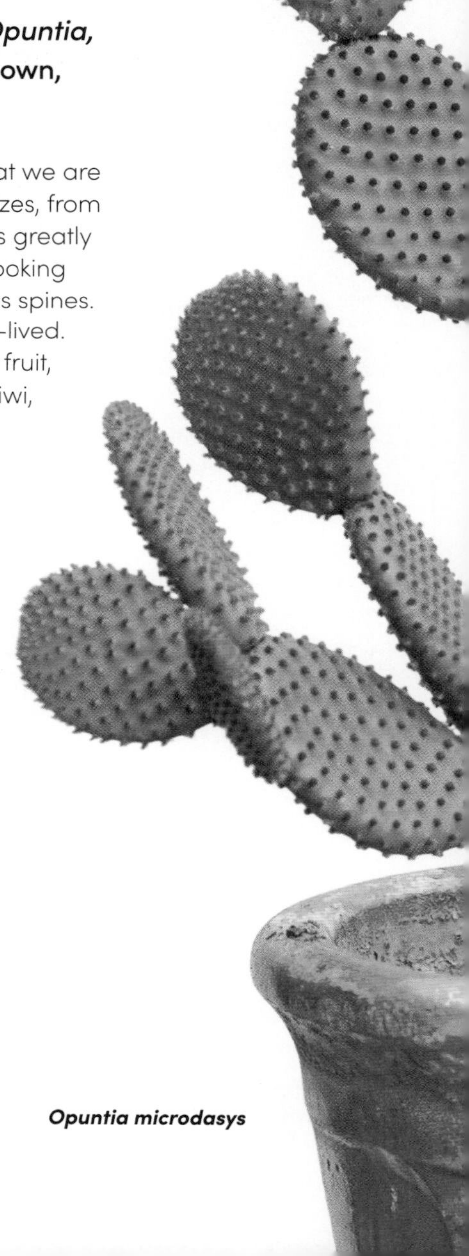

Opuntia microdasys

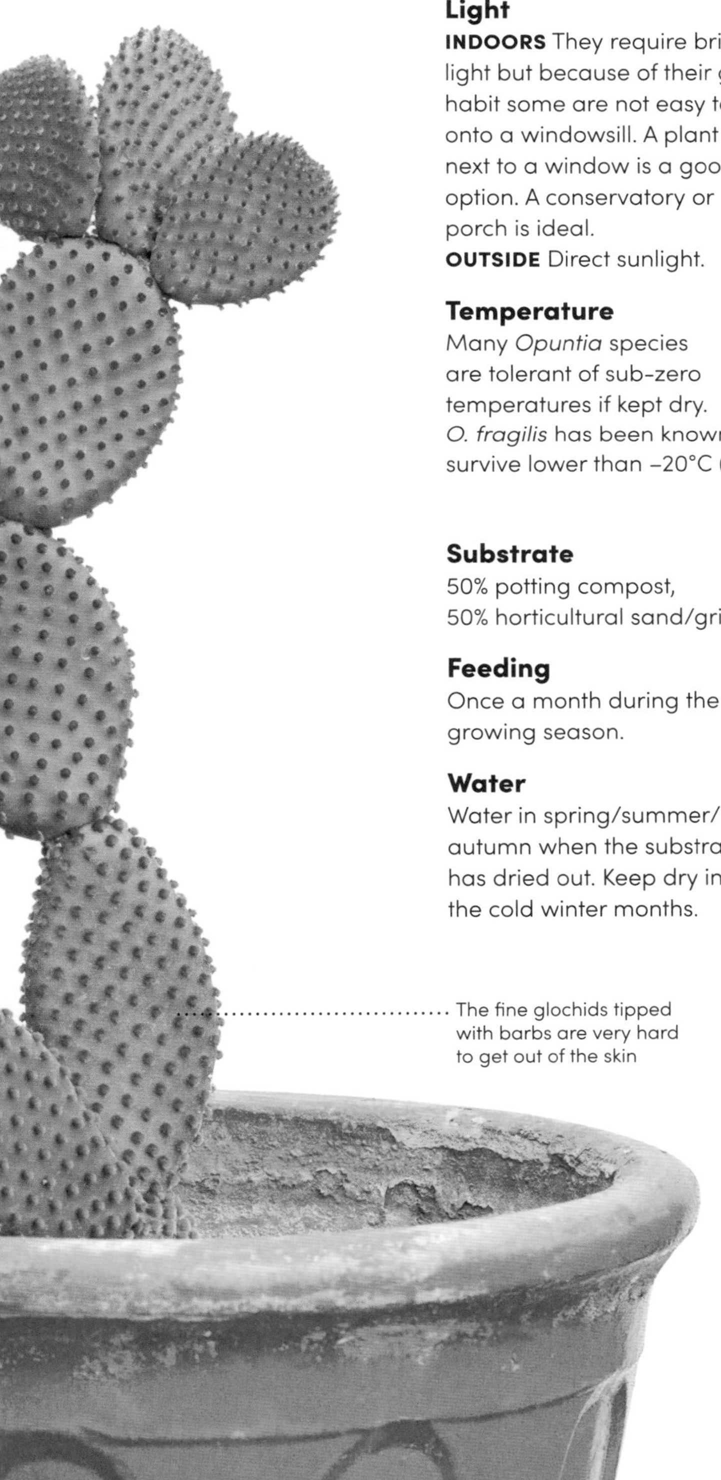

The fine glochids tipped with barbs are very hard to get out of the skin

How to grow

Light

INDOORS They require bright light but because of their growth habit some are not easy to fit onto a windowsill. A plant stand next to a window is a good option. A conservatory or porch is ideal.
OUTSIDE Direct sunlight.

Temperature

Many *Opuntia* species are tolerant of sub-zero temperatures if kept dry. *O. fragilis* has been known to survive lower than –20°C (–4°F).

Substrate

50% potting compost, 50% horticultural sand/grit.

Feeding

Once a month during the growing season.

Water

Water in spring/summer/autumn when the substrate has dried out. Keep dry in the cold winter months.

RECOMMENDED SPECIES

Opuntia monacantha* f. *monstruosa variegata
One of the very few naturally occurring variegated cacti.

O. zebrina* f. *reticulata
Also known as the cobra cactus, because of its distinctive snakeskin-like markings. Very unusual.

O. microdasys
Resembles bunny ears, which gives this species its common name. Though undoubtedly cute, this bunny has a bite in the form of glochids, which detach easily and can irritate the skin. Look, but don't touch.

O. aurea
Has a prostrate growth habit, though occasionally a single pad may grow upright. The cactus can be spineless, or may have few or multiple spines.

Parodia

Family *Cactaceae*
Subfamily *Cactoideae*
Common name Yellow ball cactus, golden ball cactus, yellow tower cactus, scarlet ball cactus, balloon cactus

Some *Parodia* plants have deeply ribbed, balloon-shaped stems

Parodia magnifica

"Beauty in diversity"

With so many different options to choose from, and many of them very easy to grow, *Parodia* is a great cactus for newbie growers.

Parodia is a complex genus in excess of 65 species, native to South America, many of which have been transferred from other genera. Because of this, there is a lot of diversity within the genus, from small, globular cacti, to tall, columnar plants reaching up to 1 metre (3¼ft) in height.

Though the stems vary greatly in appearance between species, the flowering habit is consistent. Flowers emerge from young areoles at the apex of the stem, are large and showy, and range from yellow through orange to red, pink, and purple, and sometimes green. Some species have a deeply ridged stem, whereas others have tubercles; most have dense spination.

Many *Parodia* species are suitable for beginners, with the added bonus that they flower easily – even younger plants and when grown indoors. There are some species that can be a bit more of a challenge to grow, however, so I have listed a few that I would recommend for those just starting out.

The harmless golden spines of *Parodia leninghausii* give it the common name lemon ball cactus.

How to grow

Light

INDOORS Position on a windowsill that gets a few hours of direct sunlight. Will also tolerate being on a windowsill that gets filtered sunlight.
OUTSIDE Can be grown outdoors or in a greenhouse. Shade during the hottest part of the day.

Temperature

An average minimum temperature of 5°C (41°F) is recommended for safety, although some species can tolerate lower than this for a very short period, provided they are kept bone dry and it warms up during the day.

Substrate

50% horticultural sand/grit, 50% potting compost.

Feeding

Once a month during the growing season.

Water

Allow the soil to dry out completely between waterings. Keep dry if winter days are short and cold.

RECOMMENDED SPECIES

Parodia haselbergii
A very easy-going plant and a great choice for beginners. Lovely red or yellow flowers emerge early in the year.

P. herteri
Produces beautiful pink flowers with a large yellow centre. A very easy-to-grow cactus, perfect for a sunny windowsill.

P. magnifica
Globose and clump-forming, although with age it becomes more cylindrical. Has a lovely green-blue stem with brilliant yellow flowers.

Rebutia

Family *Cactaceae*
Subfamily *Cactoideae*
Common name Crown cactus

Rebutia **is a genus of relatively small, compact globular cacti that have a clump-forming growth habit and beautiful flowers. Given their small size, they make an ideal candidate for growers with limited space.**

Native to the hills and mountains of Argentina and Bolivia, *Rebutia* is one of the most popular genera in cultivation, and its species make surprisingly easy houseplants. The number of species included in this fiercely debated genus remains a hot topic, with such genera as *Sulcorebutia*, *Weingartia*, *Aylostera*, and *Mediolobivia* now included.

The common name, crown cactus, derives from the flowers, which usually emerge in clusters around the apex of the stem, giving the impression of a crown. They are prized for their showy blooms, which, depending on the species, come in a multitude of colours – from pink, through orange and yellow, to white – and quite often will engulf the entire plant. The flowers open in the morning and close at night, and each will last for a few days.

The spines can be curved or straight, long or short, large or small, and vary between species, but they are generally soft and bristle-like. One particularly beautiful aspect of these plants is the geometric arrangement of the tubercles and spines, giving a swirled effect when viewed from above.

"Small and perfectly formed"

Rebutia heliosa

How to grow

Light

INDOORS Bright, direct light on a windowsill or in a conservatory is preferable, but they will tolerate lower light than most other cacti.
OUTSIDE Full sun or partial shade.

Temperature

An average minimum temperature of 5°C (41°F) is recommended for safety, although some species can tolerate lower than this for a very short period, provided they are kept bone dry and it warms up during the day.

Substrate

50% horticultural sand/grit, 50% potting compost.

Feeding

Once a month during the growing season.

Water

Allow the soil to dry out completely between waterings. Keep dry if winter days are short and cold.

RECOMMENDED SPECIES

Rebutia heliosa
A dwarf barrel cactus with small white thorns. Forms large clusters. The beautiful daisy-like flowers are a striking orange in spring.

R. minuscula* f. *grandiflora
The form with the largest flowers, which appear on long tubes.

R. spinosissima
Produces blood-red, delicate-looking flowers.

R. pulvinosa* subsp. *albiflora
Tiny, almost fragile in appearance, with pure white flowers.

Most species are small, globular in form, and freely produce flowers

Stenocactus

Family *Cactaceae*
Subfamily *Cactoideae*
Common name Wave cactus, brain cactus

This distinctive cactus delivers on both form and flowers, and with its globular structure made up of wavy ribs, it can indeed look a little like a brain.

Native to northern and central Mexico, *Stenocactus* are easily distinguished from other cactus genera by their deeply divided fin-like ribs that give rise to its common names. There can be up to 150 of these ribs running vertically the entire length of the plant, and their edges are home to the areoles from which the spines emerge. Depending on the species, the spines can be short, long, rigid, or pliable, and they vary in colour from white to yellow-brown to black.

The flowers emerge at the apex, are funnel-shaped, and usually white, yellow, pink, or pink with darker stripes down the centre of each petal. *Stenocactus* are mostly small, solitary, slow-growing, globular cacti reaching an average height and spread of 13cm (5in), but they can get up to about 30cm (1ft) in optimal conditions, although this is rare. There are currently 10 recognized species in the genus, and each has an impressive list of synonyms.

"Lots of names but few species"

Stenocactus crispatus

The deep, wavy ridges give rise to the common name brain cactus

How to grow

Light

INDOORS Direct sunlight on the brightest windowsill or in a conservatory.
OUTSIDE Full sun.

Temperature

An average minimum temperature of 5°C (41°F) is recommended for safety, although some species can tolerate lower than this for a very short period, provided they are kept bone dry and it warms up during the day.

Substrate

50% potting compost, 50% horticultural sand/grit/perlite.

Feeding

Once a month during the growing season.

Water

Allow the soil to dry out completely between waterings. Keep dry if winter days are short and cold.

RECOMMENDED SPECIES

Stenocactus multicostatus
The most popular and commercially available. One of the earliest-flowering cacti, usually in March/April.

S. caespitosus
Grow this one for the interesting spine formation. They curve upwards and the central spine is flattened, yellowish or pinkish.

S. crispatus
Similar to *S. multicostatus* but often has a darker stem and fewer ribs.

Tephrocactus

Family *Cactaceae*
Subfamily *Opuntioideae*
Common name Snowman cactus, pine cone cactus, paper spine cactus

---

The almost spine-free, blue-grey stem segments flush purple in the sun

Tephrocactus geometricus

"Otherworldly oddballs"

You can't help but smile and wonder at nature when you see the ball-like segments of *Tephrocactus geometricus* seemingly balancing on top of one another, giving the impression of some sort of fantastical cluster of fruit.

Native to northwestern Argentina, *Tephrocactus* is a small but distinct genus, recognizable for its idiosyncratic segments, which are cylindrical, ovate, or, in the case of *T. alexanderi* subsp. *geometricus*, spherical.

The flowers are white, pinkish, yellow, or red, but their beauty can be short-lived, with some opening for only one day. New or sun-stressed segments redden to a stunning purple colour. Some members of the genus have dramatic long spines (*T. articulatus* var. *papyracanthus*) while others possess barely visible sunken glochids. The growth habit of *Tephrocactus* makes the segments vulnerable to being knocked off. The upside is that the offsets are easy to propagate (see page 74).

Tephrocactus articulatus **is one species that has bold spines.**

How to grow

Light

INDOORS Direct sunlight on the brightest windowsill or in a conservatory.
OUTSIDE Full sun.

Temperature

An average minimum temperature of 5°C (41°F) is recommended for safety, although some species can tolerate lower than this for a very short period, provided they are kept bone dry and it warms up during the day.

Substrate

50% potting compost, 50% horticultural sand/grit/perlite.

Feeding

Once a month during the growing season.

Water

Allow the soil to dry out completely between waterings. Keep dry if winter days are short and cold.

RECOMMENDED SPECIES

Tephrocactus geometricus
Small specimens are adorable, consisting of only a few segments, resembling a snowman or a stack of juggling balls. Large specimens are awe-inspiring but expensive.

T. articulatus* var. *papyracanthus
Grow for its unusual but beautiful long, papery flattened spines.

Within the diverse cactus family, there exist forest-dwelling cacti, which break the mould entirely of the spikey, hardy plants in sun-soaked deserts that typically spring to mind. Forest cacti have adapted to both periods of drought and prolonged spells of rainfall, and, unlike their desert-dwelling relatives, they have evolved to thrive in the dense, and often shaded, understory of tropical forests.

Forest Habitat Cacti

Aporocactus

Family *Cactaceae*
Subfamily *Cactoideae*
Common name Rat tail cactus

Aporocactus flagelliformis

"Living high and occasionally dry"

Obviously named by someone who never had a good look or feel of a rat, the stems of this floriferous trailing cactus are anything but pink and soft.

Dry forests in subtropical Mexico are home to this unusual tree dweller, but although described as dry, these forests can receive hundreds of centimetres of rain per year while also experiencing long periods of drought, meaning these plants have adapted to both drought and monsoon-like rains. Here, attached to rocks or trees, is the wondrous snake-like *Aporocactus*, with its long, cascading stems that can grow up to 2 metres (6½ft) long. From each areole along the slender ribbed stems grows a cluster of short, bristle-like golden spines to protect it from predators. In spring, vivid pink, tubular flowers burst out along the stems.

The vibrant, tubular flowers appear along the stems in spring.

How to grow

Light

INDOORS Best on a sunny windowsill or hanging in a conservatory.

OUTSIDE Grow in a tall pot or hanging basket in an area that receives approximately 6 hours of dappled sunlight or in a porch. If grown in a greenhouse, allow some shade during the height of summer.

Temperature

Average minimum temperature of 5°C (41°F) is recommended for safety, although some species can tolerate lower than this provided they are kept bone dry.

Substrate

50% potting compost, 25% orchid bark, 25% sand/grit.

Feeding

Once a month during the growing season.

Water

Allow the substrate to completely dry out between waterings. Reduce the frequency in winter, allowing a longer period of dryness between waterings.

RECOMMENDED SPECIES

Aporocactus flagelliformis
This has been a staple on windowsills for many years, which is a testament to its easy-growing nature.

Aporophyllum
Not a true genus but a very attractive hybrid created by crossing *Aporocactus* with *Epiphyllum*. There is a plethora of different-coloured flowers, depending on which species have been hybridized, ranging from light pink to vivid reds.

Disocactus

Family *Cactaceae*
Subfamily *Cactoideae*
Common name Orchid cactus, red orchid cactus, fishbone cactus, strap cactus, sun cactus

A showstopping genus with long, trailing stems and a host of large, stunning bright flowers. Not one to disappoint.

Disocactus is an epiphytic (tree-dwelling) or lithophytic (growing on rock) genus of cacti, native to the tropical forests of Central America, South America, and the Caribbean. *Epiphyllum* hybrids, which are among the most commercially available jungle cacti, are derived from crosses between *Disocactus* species (rather than *Epiphyllum*) and other genera in the *Hylocereeae* tribe of cacti.

Disocactus tend to have a shrubby growth habit, with many stems, which can reach up to 3 metres (10ft) long. These can be angular, ribbed, flattened, or leaf-like. The day-blooming flowers are large and can be bright red, orange, light yellow, or white, and either funnel-shaped or tubular.

D. ackermannii, arguably the best-known species, has a confusing taxonomic history. The original specimen was lost in cultivation in the nineteenth century. Around the same time there was a successful crossing of *D. phyllanthoides* and *D. speciosus*, producing a red-flowered hybrid named *Disocactus × jenkinsonii*, and unfortunately this was cited in a publication as the original species. The true species was rediscovered in 1943, but it is rare and difficult to grow in cultivation, so most – if not all – of us who think we have a *D. ackermannii* actually have a hybrid.

The long stems have a trailing habit from growing high up in trees

"What's in a name?"

Disocactus × hybridus

When the plant matures it produces stunning large, showy flowers.

How to grow

Light

INDOORS Close to a window that receives direct sunlight only in the morning or late afternoon. They don't like direct sunlight all day. In a conservatory, provide shade. **OUTSIDE** Dappled sunlight/ semi-shade.

Temperature

Average minimum temperature of 10°C (50°F) is recommended for safety, although some species can tolerate lower than this for a very short period, provided they are kept bone dry and it warms up during the day.

Substrate

50% potting compost, 50% orchid bark/perlite/sand mix.

Feeding

Once a month during the growing season.

Water

During the growing season, allow the substrate to almost dry out before watering. In winter, if the temperature drops below 10°C (50°F), water less frequently and allow the soil to fully dry out between waterings.

RECOMMENDED SPECIES

Disocactus anguliger

Known as the fishbone cactus for its striking serrated stems, which resemble a fish skeleton. This species was formerly placed in the genus *Epiphyllum*, but according to recent molecular research, it is actually a species of *Disocactus*.

D. phyllanthoides

One of the three major species involved in creating *Epiphyllum* hybrids, with stems 1 metre (3¼ft) long and absolutely stunning large pink flowers.

D. macranthus

It's like having sunshine indoors when the beautiful, delicate yellow flowers open.

Grower profile

Jin Hyun Ahn

(with Hackney the dog, aka Hacko)

Location London, UK

Specialism Installations

Jin Hyun Ahn is the owner of Conservatory Archives, a London retailer of exotic plants that is passionate about bringing the beauty of nature into urban spaces.

When did you first become interested in cacti and succulents?

Growing up in Seoul in the 2000s, I was surrounded by mothers growing loads of succulents on their apartment balconies. Witnessing this first-hand probably instilled in me a deep familiarity with and appreciation for these chubby plants. Their resilience and beauty, with their unique architectural forms and unexpected growth patterns, left a lasting impression on me. I vividly recall the magical experience of watching my mother propagate these plants, transforming a broken piece of her *Echeveria* into over 50 new baby plants.

What inspired you to create your shop, Conservatory Archives?

Drawing inspiration from my upbringing in one of the most bustling cities, where outdoor gardening space was a rare luxury, and my immersive experience studying horticulture in the English countryside, I discovered a significant gap in indoor gardening, especially for urban dwellers. It sparked a passion to create a sanctuary that celebrates the transformative power of plants. From navigating the unpredictable British weather to immersing myself in London's vibrant creative scene, the idea for Conservatory Archives took root in 2015. The city's dynamic spirit and all the opportunities to connect with diverse individuals have been instrumental in expanding our vision and impact.

Which plants are you most proud of and why?

My affection lies with the unique specimens (not necessarily rare species) that have found a home at Conservatory Archives, each with their own story to tell. I know it is weird, but we have a collection of resident plants in our stores that are not for sale. One particular plant that holds a special place in my heart is an old *Sedum burrito*, now hanging above the shop counter. I have had this plant since 2016 in my first shop in Hackney Road. It grew a lot but then shrank to half-size and almost died hanging on the corner of the south-facing window when the shop was closed during COVID. Now it's come back to life after some intensive care. That's why I love succulents – they are true plant survivors.

Is there a common myth about growing cacti or succulents that you'd like to debunk?

I sometimes encounter the misconception that they bring bad luck or negative energy into the home. However, this myth appears to be based on cultural beliefs and superstitions in certain Asian countries. As a person of Asian descent, I challenge this myth due to the lack of scientific evidence! Cacti and succulents are not only resilient and aesthetically pleasing, but also essential for indoor garden design. Their adaptability makes them such valuable additions to indoor spaces and they really suit our busy lifestyles.

You have a unique, creative eye for plant styling. Can you give your top styling tips?

I have a keen eye for incorporating earthy and stony clay pots in various sizes. The natural texture and warmth of them add a rustic feel to a display. I also love mixing in ceramic pots with soft colours to introduce subtle pops of colour that complement the greenery as well as the furnishings and surroundings. I would say, remember that shallow pots are essential for the unique forms of those rosette-shaped, low-growing, or mounding succulents.

Epiphyllum

Family *Cactaceae*
Subfamily *Cactoideae*
Common name Orchid cactus, leaf cactus, jungle cactus, queen of the night, Dutchman's pipe cactus, princess of the night, epicacti

***Epiphyllum* is a very misunderstood genus owing to extensive hybridization, but no matter the species, its star attraction is its magnificent blooms.**

Since the early 1800s hobbyists have crossed *Epiphyllum* with other epiphytic cacti, creating a range of brightly coloured flowers. As a result there are now hundreds of different hybrids and cultivars with unclear parentage. True species – despite being labelled as "epiphyllum hybrids" or "epiphyllums" in shops – are uncommon and usually have nocturnal, white or cream, medium-to-large flowers.

The beauty of *Epiphyllum*, whether a true species or hybrid, is the flowers, which are often bigger than your hand. Cuttings from mature plants will flower, often prolifically, in the first year of growth. Epiphytes need plenty of airflow around their roots so it's best to add chunky bark to the substrate. Repotting should be done every few years as the bark breaks down, but take care not to pot on into a container that is too big, as epiphytes don't have a large root system.

"The rewards of complexity"

Ephiphyllum chrysocardium

How to grow

Light

INDOORS Epiphytes need to be close to a window that receives direct sunlight only in the morning or late afternoon. They don't like direct sunlight all day.
OUTSIDE Dappled sunlight/ semi-shade. In a greenhouse, provide shade from the midday sun.

The trailing stems of *Epiphyllum* resemble leaves

Temperature

Average minimum temperature of 10°C (50°F) is recommended for safety, although some species can tolerate lower than this for a very short period provided they are kept bone dry and it warms up during the day.

Substrate

50% potting compost, 50% orchid bark/perlite/sand mix.

Feeding

Once a month during the growing season.

Water

During the growing season, allow the substrate to almost dry out before watering. In winter, if the temperature drops below 10°C (50°F), water less frequently and allow the soil to fully dry out between waterings.

RECOMMENDED SPECIES

Epiphyllum oxypetalum
Sometimes called night-blooming cereus, which is misleading as it isn't closely related to any of the species in the tribe *Cereeae*. The spectacular white flowers bloom at night, with a lovely fragrance.

E. chrysocardium
Used to be the only species in the genus *Chiastophyllum*, in addition to a former inclusion in the genus *Selenicereus*. One of my favourite *Epiphyllum* species for the beautiful, deeply lobed stems, which resemble ferns, hence the common name fern-leaf cactus.

Any *Epiphyllum* hybrid!
All of them have stunning flowers and are very easy to grow.

Hatiora

Family *Cactaceae*
Subfamily *Cactoideae*
Common name Bottle cactus, dancing bones, spice cactus, drunkard's dream

A small genus of just three quirky epiphytic or lithophytic cacti, characterized by cross-sectioned, circular stems resembling twiglets or bones.

Hatiora salicornioides, better known as dancing bones, is native to the oceanic coastal regions of Brazil where the forests have a large number of endemic plants, which enjoy constant year-round temperatures, combined with high humidity and regular rainfall. This species was placed under the genus *Hatiora* in 1915, after previously belonging to the now-abandoned genus of *Hariota*.

H. cylindrica is native to east Brazil, where it grows in a variety of habitats, including humid forests, coastal rocks, and sometimes on dunes, and *H. herminiae* grows as an epiphyte in cloud forests in southeast Brazil at elevations of around 1,500 to 2,000 metres (4,900 to 6,600ft).

The flowers of *Hatiora* are yellow to orange or pink to magenta. Stems have a shrubby upright or trailing growth habit and dart off in every direction. The genus is closely related to *Schlumbergera* (see page 170) and *Rhipsalis* (see page 166) and is often confused with them.

Hatiora salicornioides

"Funny bones"

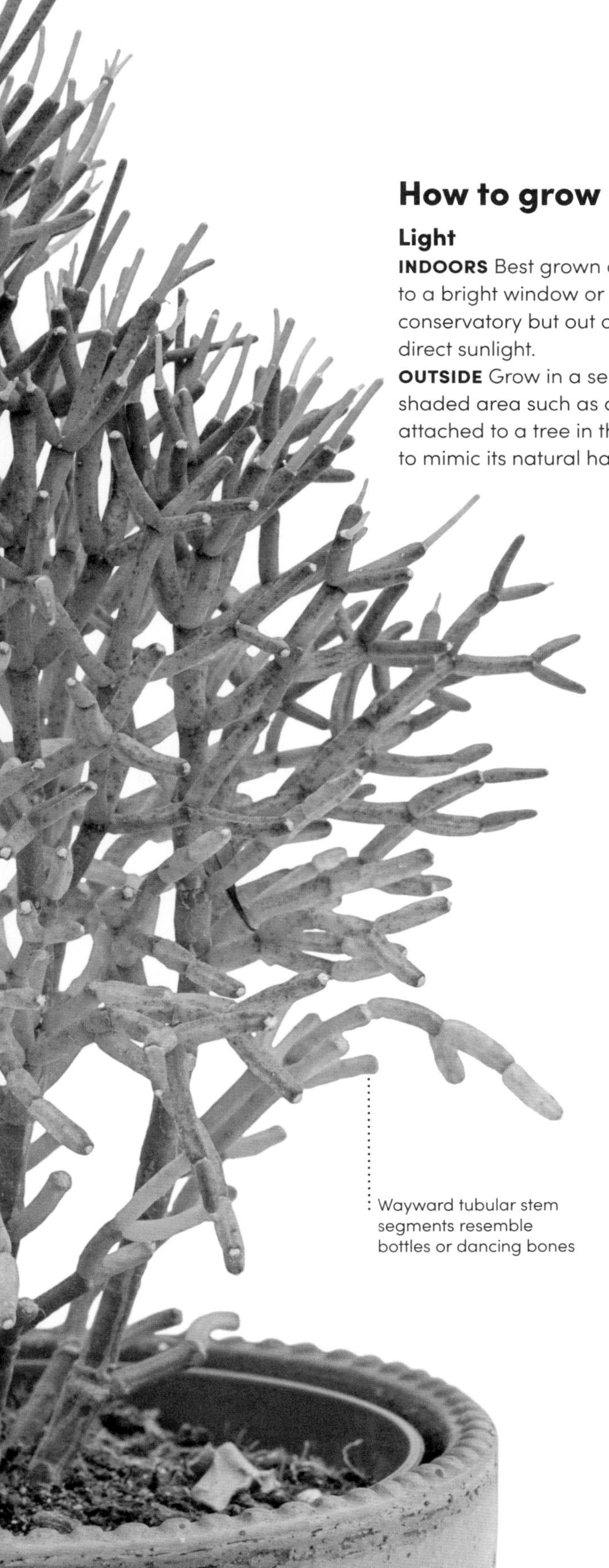

Wayward tubular stem segments resemble bottles or dancing bones

How to grow

Light

INDOORS Best grown close to a bright window or in a conservatory but out of direct sunlight.

OUTSIDE Grow in a semi-shaded area such as a porch or attached to a tree in the garden to mimic its natural habitat.

Temperature

Can tolerate an average minimum temperature of 10°C (50°F).

Substrate

50% potting compost mixed with 50% bark and grit.

Feeding

Once a month during the growing season.

Water

During the growing season, allow the substrate to almost dry out before watering. If the temperature drops below 12°C (54°F), water less frequently.

RECOMMENDED SPECIES

Hatiora salicornioides

During spring, yellow-orange, funnel-shaped flowers emerge from the tips of its segments. This is the most commonly available species; the other two species are rarely available in cultivation.

Lepismium

Family *Cactaceae*
Subfamily *Cactoideae*
Common name Hurricane cactus, snowdrop cactus

Clinging to trees in humid forests, the long, twisting, leaf-like stems of some *Lepismium* species can resemble the swirling winds of a hurricane.

Lepismium belongs to the second-largest group of cacti in Brazil, the *Rhipsalideae* tribe, which typically grow as epiphytes on tree branches (sometimes on rocks) and have long, segmented stems. *Lepismium* occurs in the forests of Argentina, Paraguay, and Brazil. Their stem segments are predominantly flat with some three-angled parts. They don't have spines, but rather some species have soft, inconspicuous, hairlike tufts growing from the areoles. The flowers are usually white, yellow, or otherwise pale coloured and appear on both sides of the stem edges.

After pollination, bright berries grow containing seeds. *Rhipsalis* (see page 166) and *Pfeiffera* (see page 162) are closely related and share similar characteristics, so if you are fond of one genus, you will likely want another from each genus. Many epiphytes, including *Lepismium*, are classified as endangered due to habitat loss from deforestation and climate change.

"Fruits of the forest"

Pendent stems vary from flat to rounded to angled

Lepismium cruciforme

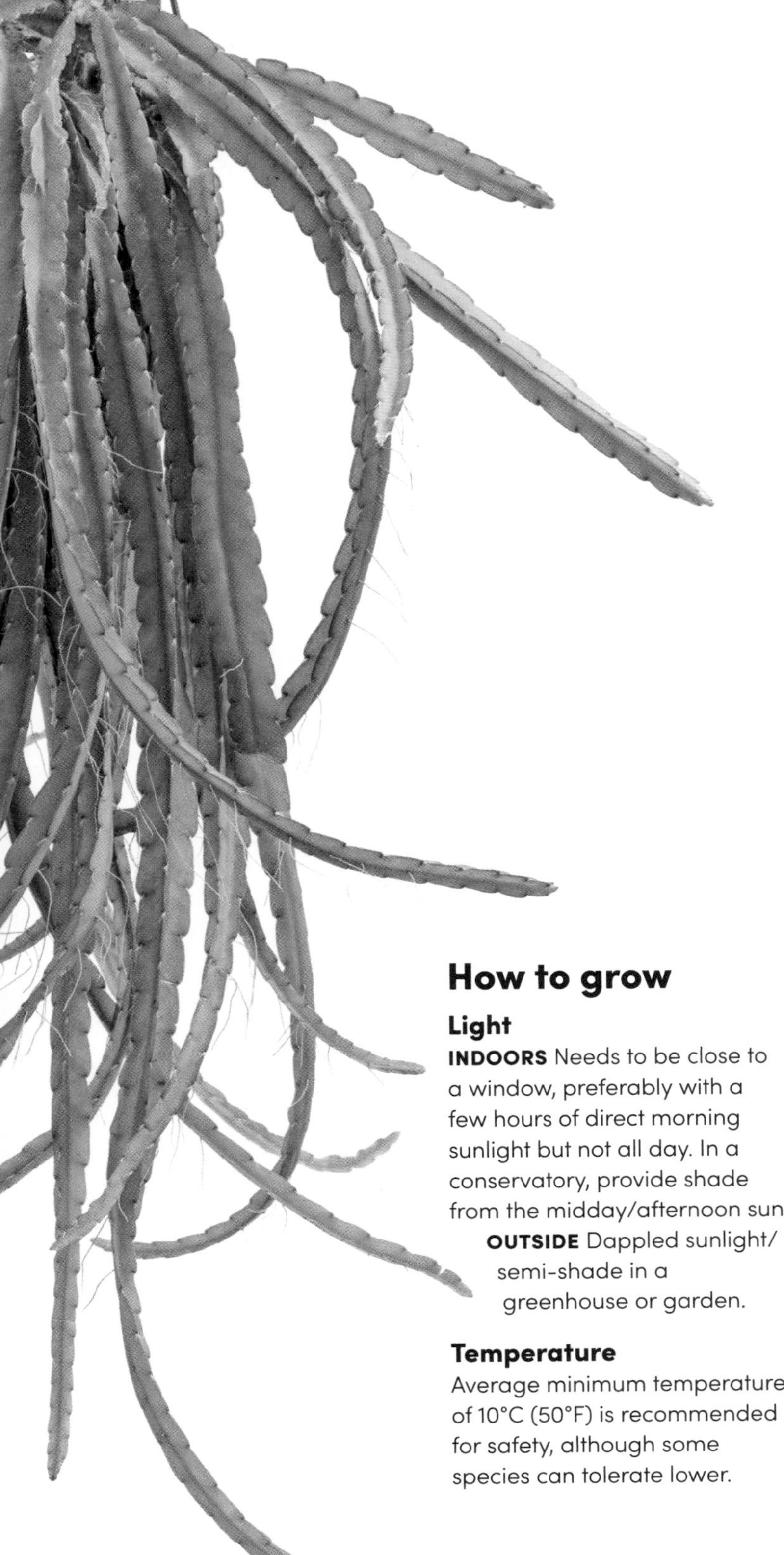

How to grow

Light

INDOORS Needs to be close to a window, preferably with a few hours of direct morning sunlight but not all day. In a conservatory, provide shade from the midday/afternoon sun.
OUTSIDE Dappled sunlight/semi-shade in a greenhouse or garden.

Temperature

Average minimum temperature of 10°C (50°F) is recommended for safety, although some species can tolerate lower.

Substrate

50% potting compost, 50% orchid bark/perlite/sand mix.

Feeding

Once a month during the growing season.

Water

During the growing season, allow the substrate to almost dry out before watering. In winter, if the temperature drops to 10°C (50°F) or below, water less frequently and allow soil to fully dry out between waterings.

RECOMMENDED SPECIES

Lepismium cruciforme
One of the most commercially available. Its long stems have scalloped edges. When stressed by cold, drought, or intense sunlight it will blush magenta. White tufts of wool grow from the submerged areoles. Easy to grow and long-lived.

L. houlletianum
The stems have joints, which give them a leaf-like appearance. The flattened stems are wider than *L. cruciforme* and the margins are roughly toothed. It flowers freely at almost any time of the year with small, creamy-yellow flowers.

L. floribundum
Floribundum means "with lots of flowers", and this plant certainly lives up to the name.

Pfeiffera boliviana

Pfeiffera

Family *Cactaceae*
Subfamily *Cactoideae*
Common name One-pined wickerware cactus

“High flyers”

***Pfeiffera* shares similar characteristics with *Lepismium* and *Rhipsalis*, and species from all three seem to regularly move from one to another.**

Pfeiffera is a small genus of mainly epiphytic, epilithic, or terrestrial plants, characterized by their flattened or angular segmented stems, which resemble leaves, giving them a distinctive appearance. The erect or pendulous stems, which branch from the middle, are known as "mesotonic" – a type of growth where the shoots nearest the middle of the stem show the greatest development. Under ideal conditions, stems are green, but most will blush a beautiful red when stressed.

The flowers are usually yellowish, orange, or white and are pollinated by insects and hummingbirds. After flowering, small, waxy berries form, containing seeds. Vivipary, a rare reproductive strategy in flowering plants in which a seed develops into a seedling before it separates from the parent plant, has been reported in only a handful of species in the *Cactaceae* family, including *P. ianthothele* and *P. monacantha*. *Pfeiffera* are most commonly found growing at altitudes from 600 metres (1,970ft) up to 2,700 metres (8,860ft), together with other epiphytes such as bromeliads and orchids.

RECOMMENDED SPECIES

Pfeiffera boliviana
As the name suggests, this species is native to Bolivia and is probably the most widely cultivated. The plant creates a curtain of arching, pendant, strap-shaped stems, reaching 1 metre (3¼ft) or more in length. There are several cultivars with different flower colours. Some are pale, others orange or even purplish.

P. monacantha
This species produces a stunning display of brightly coloured orange blooms at every areole.

***Pfeiffera monacantha* flowers appear in spring and summer.**

How to grow

Light

INDOORS Accustomed to receiving light filtered through dense, overhanging tree branches, they don't require the same light intensity as desert cacti but must be close to a window, preferably with a few hours of direct morning sunlight. In a conservatory, provide shade from the midday/ afternoon sun.

OUTSIDE Dappled sunlight/ semi-shade in a greenhouse or garden.

Temperature

Average minimum temperature of 10°C (50°F) is recommended for safety, although some species can tolerate lower than this for a short period.

Substrate

50% potting compost, 50% orchid bark/perlite/sand mix.

Feeding

Once a month during the growing season.

Water

During the growing season, allow the substrate to almost dry out before watering. In winter, if the temperature drops to 10°C (50°F) or below, water less frequently and allow soil to fully dry out between waterings.

Rhipsalidopsis

Family *Cactaceae*
Subfamily *Cactoideae*
Common name Easter cactus, holiday cactus, Whitsun cactus

***Rhipsalidopsis gaertneri* hybrid**

The Easter cactus can be recognized from its star-shaped flowers

"A spring treat"

It would be fair to say that few people have heard of the dinosaur-like name *Rhipsalidopsis*, and yet millions of people own one.

Rhipsalidopsis takes its name from the similar genus *Rhipsalis* (see page 166) and the Greek word *opsis*, meaning "appearance". Although *Rhipsalidopsis* currently comprises only two species, it is arguably one of the most popular genera, owing to its major player, *R. gaertneri*, the Easter cactus. The common name reflects the period in which it flowers in the northern hemisphere, namely late spring, but it can flower twice a year.

R. gaertneri has been hybridized with the other member of the genus, *R. rosea*, a pink-flowered species, to form the hybrid *Rhipsalidopsis* × *graeseri*, cultivars of which have many different-coloured flowers. *R. rosea* grows as an epiphyte in the cloud forests of south Brazil and is listed as near threatened due to deforestation. Its segmented stems branch in a "Y" shape and each cladode has areoles at the tips where the pink flowers emerge. *R. gaertneri* is characterized by flattened, rounded cladodes, sometimes with a pronounced darker-coloured edge, which makes it easily distinguishable from the Christmas or Thanksgiving cactus belonging to the genus *Schlumbergera* (see page 170), to which *Rhipsalidopsis* is closely related.

RECOMMENDED SPECIES

Rhipsalidopsis gaertneri
The Easter cactus is considered more difficult to grow than the Christmas or Thanksgiving cactus (see page 170). However, I treat them more or less the same and have success. They are perhaps more sensitive to overwatering, so to counteract this I use a terracotta pot.

R. rosea
Rare in cultivation and the wild. A beautiful plant but it's unlikely you'll find it in your local garden centre. I was very lucky to be gifted one by grower Mellie Lewis, who features on page 182.

How to grow

Light

INDOORS Must be close to a window, preferably with a few hours of direct morning or afternoon sunlight. In a conservatory, provide shade from the midday/afternoon sun.
OUTSIDE Dappled sunlight/semi-shade in a greenhouse or garden.

Temperature

Average minimum temperature of 10°C (50°F) is recommended for safety, although some species can tolerate lower than this for a short period.

Substrate

50% potting compost, 50% orchid bark/perlite/sand mix.

Feeding

Once a month during the growing season.

Water

During the growing season, allow the substrate to almost dry out before watering. In winter, if the temperature drops to 10°C (50°F) or below, water less frequently and allow soil to fully dry out between waterings.

In most species, spines are missing or occur only in the juvenile stage

Rhipsalis

Family *Cactaceae*
Subfamily *Cactoideae*
Common name Mistletoe cactus, coral cactus

A highly unusual cactus in looks, kind, and character. Tolerant of less light than other cacti, *Rhipsalis* makes the perfect houseplant for those looking to add a bit of drama to a room.

Rhipsalis is a fascinating genus of cacti for a few reasons. Firstly, the species bear little resemblance to typical cacti; most are spineless, and unlike all other species of cacti, one member, *R. baccifera*, is native to both the Americas and Africa, making it the only cactus native to somewhere other than the Americas. In forests ranging from coastal habitats to almost 3,000 metres (9,850ft) altitude, *Rhipsalis* are primarily epiphytic, living in trees, but some are lithophytic and grow in rocky crevices.

Their stems resemble flattened leaves and can be cylindrical, segmented, angular, or jointed, with a cascading or pendulous growth habit, which makes them suitable for hanging baskets. Their flowers are small and inconspicuous but very pretty, usually white or cream in colour. After flowering, small, berry-like fruits appear, hence the name mistletoe cactus.

"A cactus unlike any other"

Rhipsalis pilocarpa

The star-burst flowers of *Rhipsalis pilocarpa* are small but abundant.

How to grow

Light

INDOORS Accustomed to receiving light filtered through dense, overhanging tree branches, they don't require the same light intensity as desert cacti but must be close to a window, preferably with a few hours of direct morning sunlight. In a conservatory, provide shade from the midday/ afternoon sun.
OUTSIDE Dappled sunlight/ semi-shade in a greenhouse or garden.

Temperature

Average minimum temperature of 10°C (50°F) is recommended for safety, although some species can tolerate lower than this for a short period.

Substrate

50% potting compost, 50% orchid bark/perlite/sand mix.

Feeding

Once a month during the growing season.

Water

During the growing season, allow the substrate to almost dry out before watering. In winter, if the temperature drops below 10°C (50°F), water less frequently and allow the soil to fully dry out between waterings.

RECOMMENDED SPECIES

Rhipsalis baccifera
Has long, cascading, spaghetti-like stems, and when in fruit the glistening white berries look similar to those of mistletoe.

R. pilocarpa
Long, hairy branching stems and stunning tiny flowers make the plant look as if it's decorated in fairy lights.

Grower profile

Ian Woolnough

Location Near King's Lynn, Norfolk

Specialism Growing cacti from seed

Membership British Cactus and Succulent Society, Mammillaria Society, ELK Cactus Society

Ian's saguaro (*Carnegia gigantea*) is thought to be the only specimen that flowers in the UK.

Ian is a cartographer and geologist who has travelled widely in the Americas in search of cacti. He is the owner of the former Eau Brink Cactus Nursery in Norfolk, and has written articles and spoken internationally on cacti.

Ian alongside just some of his vast collection.

Which plant in your collection are you most proud of and why?

A *Blossfeldia* the size of a 10p piece on its own roots that I grew from seed. They are small, slow, and easily swamped by moss, so I was chuffed to work out a way of growing them successfully without grafting.

What's been your biggest failure, and what did you learn from it?

One year I sowed a load of old seed I'd been given and none of it germinated. Seed such as *Astrophytum* or *Frailea* needs to be sown when as fresh as possible, and at least before it is three years old.

What substrate do you use for most of your plants?

I have specific mixes for different plants, but they can be broken down broadly into three types. For Chilean plants and some North American plants (*Copiapoa, Eriosyce, Sclerocactus*) I use a very free-draining, gritty mix with no l imestone but some humus and sand. For *Astrophytum, Turbinicarpus*, white-spined *Mammillaria*, etc., I have a limestone mix with some humus and grit, and for general potting I have a loam, grit, and John Innes mix.

Is there a common myth about growing cacti or succulents that you'd like to debunk?

Yes – that they rarely flower, as with the right care most species will flower readily. Also, growing them from seed is much easier than people expect.

How do you water during the different seasons?

I generally stop watering in November and don't start again until February or March, depending on the weather. However, looking at the plant often shows when they need water. I don't water when it is very hot and am careful not to water from above if it is going to be sunny, as they can scorch. For many plants, such as *Ariocarpus*, I don't water in the summer, as in habitat they rarely receive rain then and seem to benefit from a rest when it is hot.

What advice would you give beginners?

Experiment. Everyone's growing conditions are different so what might work for someone else won't necessarily work for you. Make sure plants have sufficient light (although epiphytic cacti need more shading) and, if possible, go to a local British Cactus and Succulent Society (BCSS) meeting, where you'll meet like-minded people and learn from their experiences – and very likely you'll be able to source plants that you were completely unaware of at reasonable prices, or even for free.

Five plants everyone should grow?

1. ***Thelocactus bicolor.*** It's easy to grow and produces fantastic showy flowers even when quite small.

2. ***Mammillaria surculosa.*** Again, easy to grow, and the freely produced yellow flowers are pleasantly citrus-scented.

3. ***Astrophytum** hybrids.* Especially *A. myriostigma* 'Onzuka', as they look great all year round, with fantastic flocking and patterns on the bodies.

4. ***Turbinicarpus.*** It doesn't really matter which species as they all flower when small and never take up too much space.

5. ***Weingartia.*** This plant produces an incredible number of flowers and is not overly demanding.

What are your top tips for plant care?

Use rainwater when possible, add extra-sharp grit to any potting mix to help with drainage, and ensure enough light to prevent etiolation (pale, leggy growth) but not too much when hot and sunny to prevent scorch, unless there is good air movement. Take into account where the plants are from when deciding what conditions they are likely to need.

Mammillaria lenta **flowering well in a small pot.**

Schlumbergera × buckleyi

The segmented stem sections are known as cladodes

Schlumbergera

Family *Cactaceae*
Subfamily *Cactoideae*
Common name Christmas cactus, Thanksgiving cactus

"A lifelong commitment, not just for Christmas"

You may not know the name *Schlumbergera*, but you've probably heard of holiday cacti. More than just seasonal decoration, these plants can be long-lived and are often passed down through generations (see page 68).

As its common name implies, the *Schlumbergera × buckleyi* hybrid usually flowers in mid-winter, over the Christmas season, and its close relative the Thanksgiving cactus (*Schlumbergera truncata* hybrid) tends to flower earlier, in line with Thanksgiving. However, the flowering periods can fluctuate wildly from plant to plant, depending on their environment, which can leave the owner confused as to the true identity of their plant.

There are several ways to differentiate between these two hybrids: the cladodes are shaped differently, and the pollen (not the flowers) is different colours. The Thanksgiving cactus has pointed teeth at the end of each segment and yellow pollen, whereas the Christmas cactus has rounded scalloped-shaped segments and pink pollen. The Easter cactus belongs to the genus *Rhipsalidopsis* (see page 164), and has rounded cladodes and radially symmetrical flowers that look like starbursts.

Sadly, the Christmas cactus fell out of favour with commercial growers and is rarely produced any more. If you're looking to buy a true Christmas cactus, search for one second-hand; there are some stunning old beauties available.

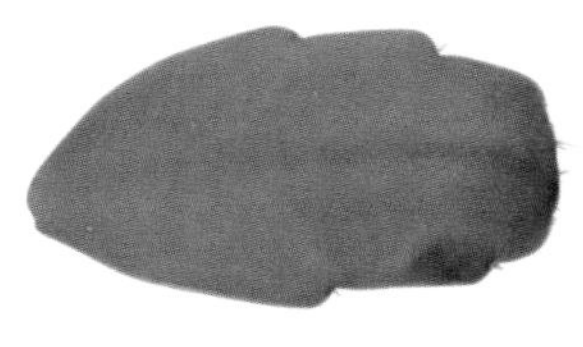

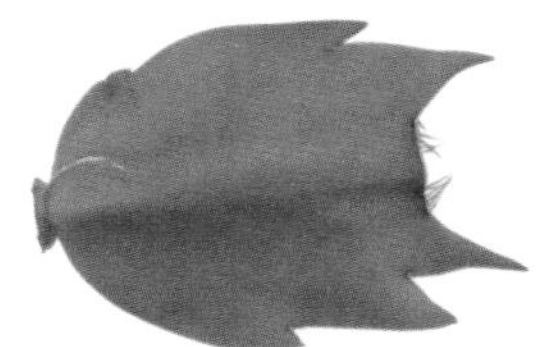

Which holiday cactus do you have? Christmas (top), Thanksgiving (middle), or Easter (bottom)?

How to grow

Light

INDOORS Best grown close to a window, but out of direct sunlight.

OUTSIDE In a semi-shaded area such as a porch or attached to a tree in the garden to mimic its natural habitat.

Temperature

Average minimum temperature of 10°C (50°F) is recommended for safety, although some species can tolerate lower than this for a short period.

Substrate

50% potting compost, 50% bark and grit.

Feeding

Once a month during the growing season.

Water

During the growing season, allow the substrate to almost dry out before watering. In winter water less frequently if the temperature drops to 10°C (50°F) or below and allow soil to fully dry out between waterings.

RECOMMENDED SPECIES

Schlumbergera × buckleyi
Many different cultivars are available on websites such as eBay, Facebook Marketplace, and Etsy.

***S. truncata* hybrids**
Commonly known as the Thanksgiving cactus, these come in a wide variety of colours and many will flower more than once a year.

Selenicereus

Family *Cactaceae*
Subfamily *Cactoideae*
Common name Moonlight cactus, queen of the night, princess of the night, fishbone cactus, ric rac cactus, zigzag cactus, orchid cactus

Using aerial roots to scramble across rocks and climb trees, *Selenicereus* stems can grow many metres long, but the real showstopper are the flowers, which will keep you up all night.

Native to the forests of Mexico, the Caribbean, and northern South America, *Selenicereus* is a genus of epiphytic (tree-dwelling), hemi-epiphytic (germinating on a host tree but later establishing root contact with the soil), lithophytic (rock-dwelling), and terrestrial cacti. The name derives from Selene, the moon goddess in Greek and Roman religion, and *Cereus*, the genus it used to belong to. The moon in this case refers to the stunning flowers that open at night to be pollinated by moths and in some cases bats. The blooms emerge from elongated shoots towards the stem tips and are large, showy, and usually white, with an intense fragrance. Sadly, they usually only last for one night.

There are currently 28 species in the genus. Perhaps the best-known is *S. undatus*, which produces the white-fleshed pitahaya. It is grown both as an ornamental vine and as a fruit crop – known as dragon fruit. The stems are cylindrical, flattened, or dramatically angled like *S. anthonyanus*, which has alternating, triangular lobes and is commonly known as the zigzag or ric rac cactus (not to be confused with *Epiphyllum anguliger*, which has the same common names).

"For one night only"

Selenicereus grandiflorus

How to grow

Light

INDOORS Close to a window that gets only a few hours of direct sunlight a day.
OUTSIDE Dappled sunlight/semi-shade.

Temperature

Average minimum temperature of 5°C (41°F) is recommended, although some species can tolerate lower than this for a very short period, if kept dry and it warms up during the day.

Substrate

50% potting compost, 50% orchid bark/perlite/sand mix.

Feeding

Once a month during the growing season.

Water

During the growing season, allow to almost dry out before watering. In winter, if light levels drop and it falls to 10°C (50°F) or below, water less frequently and allow soil to fully dry out between waterings.

RECOMMENDED SPECIES

Selenicereus anthonyanus
The serrated stems and huge pinkish flowers are stunning.

S. validus
Beautiful pendant plant with rope-like stems.

S. grandiflorus
The true species is rare in cultivation but there are some very nice hybrids. *Grandiflorus* is Latin for "large flowered".

While all cacti are succulents, not all succulents are cacti, and therefore they require their own subsection. They encompass an astonishing variety of shapes, sizes, and colours, with species native to many different habitats around the world, from the African deserts to the mountains of southern Europe. Understanding the distinctions between succulents and cacti, and the climates they inhabit, is crucial for their care.

Succulents

Adenium

Family *Apocynaceae*
Subfamily *Apocynoideae*
Common name Desert rose, mock azalea

Adenium obesum

"Not all roses have thorns"

Adenium flowers are among the showiest of all succulents, ranging from pink to red, and can bloom for months, making them an appealing houseplant.

Adeniums, referred to as "desert roses", are known for their vibrant flowers and thick, unusual caudices. They are native to the arid lands of the Sahel, sub-Saharan Africa, and the Arabian peninsula, where these bloated beauties are found growing in sandy soil in sunny, open areas. The species range from shrublets with underground or exposed caudices to tree-like plants with bulbous trunks and stems reaching up to 5 metres (16½ft) in height. They are often used for bonsai because of their stunning flowers and swollen, woody stems, which create the most spectacular shapes, particularly when the roots are exposed above the soil. Don't be alarmed if in winter they drop all their leaves; this is perfectly normal as the plant enters dormancy.

The leaves can drop from this bonsai-like plant when dormant

How to grow

Light

INDOORS On a bright windowsill that receives at least a few hours of direct sunlight.
OUTSIDE In an unshaded position in a greenhouse or garden in full sun. Perfect in a pot on a bright patio or deck.

Temperature

In winter, best kept in temperatures no lower than 10°C (50°F).

Substrate

60% potting compost,
40% horticultural sand/grit.

Feeding

Once or twice a month in the growing season.

Water

In spring/summer water when the substrate has completely dried out. If, in winter, the plant goes dormant, water only once or twice until next spring.

RECOMMENDED SPECIES

Adenium obesum
This species has the most beautiful, fancy flowers.

A. arabicum
A subspecies of *A. obesum*. If you are mostly interested in the form of the plant caudex, you should look for this one.

Adromischus

Family *Crassulaceae*
Subfamily *Kalanchoideae*
Common name Plover eggs plant

Diminutive, alienesque succulents boasting a variety of intriguing textures and colours, often speckled or mottled with curious patterns.

The genus *Adromischus* is native to dry, rocky areas of southern Africa. The leaves are tactile and can be fuzzy, smooth, or crinkled, and tubular or egg-like in shape. *A. marianiae* var. *hallii* looks so much like little bird's eggs you would be forgiven for looking around for the nest from which they've fallen. If you've ever seen a plover's eggs, you'll know why it's used as the common name for *A. cooperi*.

Most *Adromischus* grow during spring and late summer through to autumn when the days are cooler. During the height of summer and the cold, dark days of winter they prefer a dryer "resting" period. The flowers are delicate and understated, emerging on tall, slender stalks in summer. They are typically small, tubular, and pale, providing a contrast to the unusual bold leaves. *Adromischus* cultivars can fetch a high price. The stranger looking, the better.

"Nest eggs"

Adromischus maculatus

How to grow

Light

INDOORS On a warm, bright windowsill with early morning or late-afternoon direct sunlight.
OUTSIDE *Adromischus* generally grow at the base of large shrubs or in the shade of rocks where they receive plenty of light while still being protected from some of the sun's harshness. They would do well in a sunny or semi-shaded rock garden. Provide some shade in a greenhouse.

Temperature

Average minimum temperature of 5°C (41°F) is recommended for safety, although some species can tolerate lower than this for a very short period, provided they are kept bone dry and it warms up during the day.

Substrate

50% potting compost,
50% horticultural sand/grit.

Feeding

During the growing period, feed once or twice a month.

Water

Water during the growing period when the substrate is completely dry. Give little or none when resting.

Stems have unique forms and patterns, such as marbling or spots

Adromischus marianae var. *hallii* looks remarkably like a bird's eggs.

RECOMMENDED SPECIES

Adromischus marianiae* f. *herrei
Has fat ovate or round leaves, chalky grey-green, which are either red-spotted or plain.

A. cooperi
One of the most commonly grown, with nice, fat, purple-speckled, silvery-green to blue-green leaves.

Aeonium

Family *Crassulaceae*
Subfamily *Sempervivoideae*
Common name Tree houseleek

Aeoniums are one of my all-time favourite succulents for their ease of care, sculptural appearance, and beautiful flower-like heads.

Aeonium is a group of relatively fast-growing species native to areas of northern Africa and nearby islands, including the Canary Islands, Cape Verde, and Madeira. Despite their native warm, temperate habitats, these hardy succulents feature in many gardens in Cornwall, UK, where they happily tolerate low temperatures and a lot of rain. Mature species can become almost tree-like, with twisting stems reaching 1.5 metres (5ft) or more, on top of which are heads of tight rosette-formation leaves.

Mature rosettes produce conical clusters of small, star-shaped flowers, which may be creamy-white, yellowish, golden, pink, or red, depending on the species or cultivar. *Aeonium* species are monocarpic, which means they die after flowering. If a branching variety flowers, only the rosette that produced the flower will die, and the rest of the plant will live. A branching species will continue to grow after flowering, while single-headed species will die but can be propagated by seed.

"A winning rosette"

***Aeonium arboreum* 'Atropurpureum'**

The glossy, evergreen, waxy leaves form a beautiful rosette

How to grow

Light

INDOORS These plants can become leggy indoors, with small rosettes of leaves. Best kept right next to the brightest, biggest window or in a conservatory.

OUTSIDE Keep them in pots so they can be easily moved indoors or into a greenhouse if it gets cold. They can tolerate low temperatures but can rot in cold, damp conditions.

Temperature

Average minimum temperature 5°C (41°F).

Substrate

75% horticultural sand/grit/pumice, 25% potting compost.

Feeding

Once or twice during the growing season.

Water

Aeoniums often enter a dormant phase in the summer, characterized by tighter rosettes and the shedding of outer leaves. During this period, they require less water. Keep dry if temperatures drop.

RECOMMENDED SPECIES

Aeonium arboreum

This tree-form species comes in a variety of colours, ranging from green to the striking, almost-black 'Zwartkop'.

A. tabuliforme

Known as the saucer plant, this sadly dies after flowering at about three years old, but it's worth growing to marvel at the tight, flat, spiral formation of the leaves. Sometimes, the centre of the plant becomes crested, making it look even more bizarre.

A. haworthii

Also known as Haworth's aeonium or pinwheel. Produces many offsets, forming a dense, compact mound. In spring, some of the mature rosettes produce cream-coloured, pointed flowers.

Grower profile

Mellie Lewis

Locations Clun, Shropshire, UK

Specialism National Collection of Aeoniums

Mellie is the proud owner of the UK's National Collection of Aeoniums. She has been growing plants for over 40 years and makes regular expeditions to see aeoniums and other succulents in habitat. She is a writer and speaker, and has won numerous medals for her exhibits at RHS shows and festivals.

Why did you want to have the National Collection of Aeoniums?

It wasn't until 2018 and a chance meeting with the Plant Heritage Shropshire coordinator who encouraged me to apply for the National Collection. In 2019 I was awarded the status – this was a first; nobody had ever had a NC of aeoniums before me. I felt very proud of my plants and have been on a mission ever since to get the genus in the limelight! I currently have over 300 different varieties, made up of species, interspecific hybrids, and cultivars.

Which plant are you most proud of and why?

I'm going to choose *Aeonium* 'Bronze Teacup' – a gorgeous cultivar, introduced from the US in 2006, but it quickly became forgotten, as it doesn't offset readily and is a slow grower. In 2020, I entered the plant into the RHS/Plant Heritage Threatened Plant of the Year competition, and it won the People's Choice vote. This has bounced the plant back into cultivation and aeonium enthusiasts have sourced the plant for their collections, which is great news. It's such a beauty and I'm so pleased it has not been lost to history!

How do you care for aeoniums during the different seasons?

Aeoniums are tender plants, make no mistake; they cannot tolerate frosts! They need overwintering in a frost-free, well-ventilated, light place. Keep on the dry side until early spring. During cold weather check them daily – they might need extra care, like a fleece covering. Not all aeoniums enjoy full sun either; this can cause them to go into dormancy, and if this happens and we get a rainstorm, it can rot the plant. It's best during the summer months to place them where they can get a few hours of strong sunlight but then go into shade.

What is your advice on watering?

Follow the three Ds: drench, drain, dry. Only water when dried out, then give a good drenching, before leaving until completely dry again.

Five of the best easy-care aeoniums?

1. ***Aeonium* 'Zwartkop'**. Makes a large arboreum plant of dark-purple rosettes

2. ***A.* 'Kiwi'**. A beautiful plant of shrubby habit with colourful cream, lime-green, and pink rosettes.

3. ***A. arboreum* 'Atropurpureum'**. A plant that forms a small tree shape. Leaves are green in winter, changing to purple in spring, summer, and autumn. An easy plant to take cuttings from.

4. ***A. tabuliforme*.** A species from Tenerife, which grows into a dinner-plate-sized flat rosette of stunning formation. A talking point, although short-lived.

5. ***A.* 'Velour'**. A beautiful cultivar with velvet leaves in purples and reds. Easy to grow, and happy in a summer planter display.

The beautifully tinged *Aeonium* 'Copper Kettle' – a quick grower, great for beginners.

Aeonium tabuliforme – its densely formed rosette is a wonder to behold.

Aeonium 'Medusa', with its stunning variegation.

Vintage wooden ladders make a lovely display for miniature-type aeoniums.

Agave

Family *Asparagaceae*
Subfamily *Agavoideae*
Common name Century plant, American aloe

A plant of many uses and striking architectural beauty, *Agave* definitely earns its place as a must-have succulent.

Agave plants originate from the arid areas of the Americas, the Caribbean, and Mexico. Inhabiting a diverse range of habitats from grasslands to pine woods, they are defined by their rosettes of tough, sword-like leaves, which are often edged with formidable thorns. Most *Agave* are monocarpic; each rosette flowers only once and then dies. Only a small number of species are polycarpic, blooming multiple times during their lifetime.

When an *Agave* flowers, you certainly know about it; it sends up a towering flower stalk that can reach 12 metres (39¼ft) high. The flowers, arranged in elaborate panicles, vary in colour and are rich in nectar, attracting pollinators from bats to bees. Not only are these stunning architectural plants, but for centuries they have also played an important role in human culture as a source of fibre for fabric and food, soap for washing clothes, shoe polish, and a potent drink, with the blue agave famous for its role in producing tequila.

"The only plant that can get you drunk and polish your shoes"

Agave victoriae-reginae

The thick, succulent leaves have pointed tips and often serrated edges

How to grow

Light

INDOORS They require bright light but because of their growth habit they're not easy to fit onto a windowsill. A plant stand next to a window is a good option. A conservatory or porch is ideal.
OUTSIDE Direct sunlight.

Temperature

Many species are tolerant of sub-zero temperatures. Those native to desert, arid, and mountainous regions are more cold-tolerant than those from tropical or subtropical regions. For safety a minimum of 5°C (41°F) is suggested.

Substrate

50% potting compost,
50% horticultural sand/grit.

Feeding

During the growing period feed once or twice a month.

Water

Water when the substrate has totally dried out. Keep dry in the cold winter months.

RECOMMENDED SPECIES

Agave americana
Has blue-green leaves, which can reach an impressive size. Iconic – a must-have.

***A. americana* 'Variegata'**
The striking yellow-edged leaves add sculptural interest to a planted bed.

A. victoriae-reginae
Has a beautiful domed formation with leaves edged in white. Impossibly stunning.

A. montana
Forms a solitary rosette of dark-green leaves that are lined with small, sharp teeth. It is well suited to cooler climates and can tolerate frost.

Aloe

Family *Asphodelaceae*
Subfamily *Asphodeloideae*
Common name First aid plant

Prized for its medicinal properties as well as its stylish structure, *Aloe* is a star of the succulent world.

There are close to 600 species of *Aloe* native to tropical and southern Africa, Madagascar, Jordan, the Arabian Peninsula, and various islands in the Indian Ocean, where they thrive in a range of habitats, including deserts, grasslands, coastal areas, and even alpine regions. The genus is diverse in size and growth habit. Small species have radial rosettes growing directly at ground level, while others form a trunk or stem, either solitary or branched. Larger species are not suitable for indoor growing.

Flowers vary in colour from near white to yellow, orange, and almost red, and most grow on top of tall, single or branched stalks, which are rigid enough to support birds who explore the flowers for nectar. A few species have short-tubed, whitish or cream flowers, such as *A. inconspicua*, which are pollinated by insects. *Aloe* has a long ethnobotanical and medicinal history centred around the ubiquitous *A. vera*. By far the best-known species, it has been used for centuries for a wide range of purposes, including as a treatment for psoriasis, burns, and sores, and as a tonic to aid digestion.

“A soothing sensation”

Fleshy *Aloe* leaves are often edged with contrasting spiky teeth

Aloe brevifolia

How to grow

Light

INDOORS Most like a spot on the brightest windowsill, but *A. vera* is less tolerant of direct sun and prefers a few hours in the morning. In a conservatory, provide shade from the midday/afternoon sun.

OUTSIDE Larger specimens thrive in full sun; smaller ones require semi-shade.

Temperature

Average minimum temperature of 5°C (41°F) is recommended for safety, although some species can tolerate lower than this for a very short period, provided they are kept bone dry and it warms up during the day.

Substrate

50% potting compost,
50% horticultural sand/grit.

Feeding

Once a month during the growing season.

Water

Allow the substrate to completely dry out between waterings. If you experience cold winters, don't water at all during this season.

The delicate orange flowers of *Aloe striata* lend it the common name coral aloe.

RECOMMENDED SPECIES

Aloe ferox
Has dark spines resembling thorns along the margins of the leaves. Striking appearance.

A. perfoliata
Formerly known as *A. mitriformis*, this clump-forming species has attractive reddish-green leaves and yellow spine-like growths.

A. arborescens
A large *Aloe*, best grown outside in the garden or a pot. It has dense rosettes of toothed leaves, from which torch-like red flowers grow in summer.

A. rauhii
Also known as snowflake aloe, this small species forms rosettes of triangular, pale-green leaves with white patterning and tiny teeth along the margins. It produces offsets around the base and creates mounding clumps.

***Aloiampelos striatula* (syn. *A. striatula*)**
A hardy *Aloe* suitable for colder regions. It has a sprawling growth habit and can climb if given support. The leaves are striped in different shades of green and the flower spike is tall and dramatic.

Ceropegia

Family *Apocynaceae*
Subfamily *Asclepiadoideae*
Common name String of hearts, chain of hearts, collar of hearts, lantern flower, necklace vine, parachute flower, wine-glass vine

---

This genus is best known for the ubiquitous string of hearts species (*Ceropegia woodii*), loved for its small, pretty leaves that adorn the long, string-like stems. However, my fascination lies with the flowers...

The flowers of *Ceropegia* are a true wonder, often fused at several points to form a cage or umbrella-like structure, and many bear similarities to carrion flowers or stapelias, mimicking animal-related odours or rotting plant material because it is used as food substrate by the larvae of some flies. Some literally hold their pollinators captive. Lured by chemical signals, flies or gnats enter the extraordinarily shaped flowers and are prevented from escaping until they have feasted on the nectar and inadvertently covered themselves with pollen. Within a day or so, the flower withers, and the pollinator is freed, carrying the precious cargo.

The genus is as varied in its habitats as it is in morphology, being found in environments ranging from deserts to misty mountains in countries across southern Africa to northeast Australia. Many species, including *C. woodii*, are sold as hanging plants despite scrambling across the ground or climbing up through vegetation, their often-tuberous roots allowing them to withstand periods of drought.

"Captivating hearts"

Ceropegia woodii

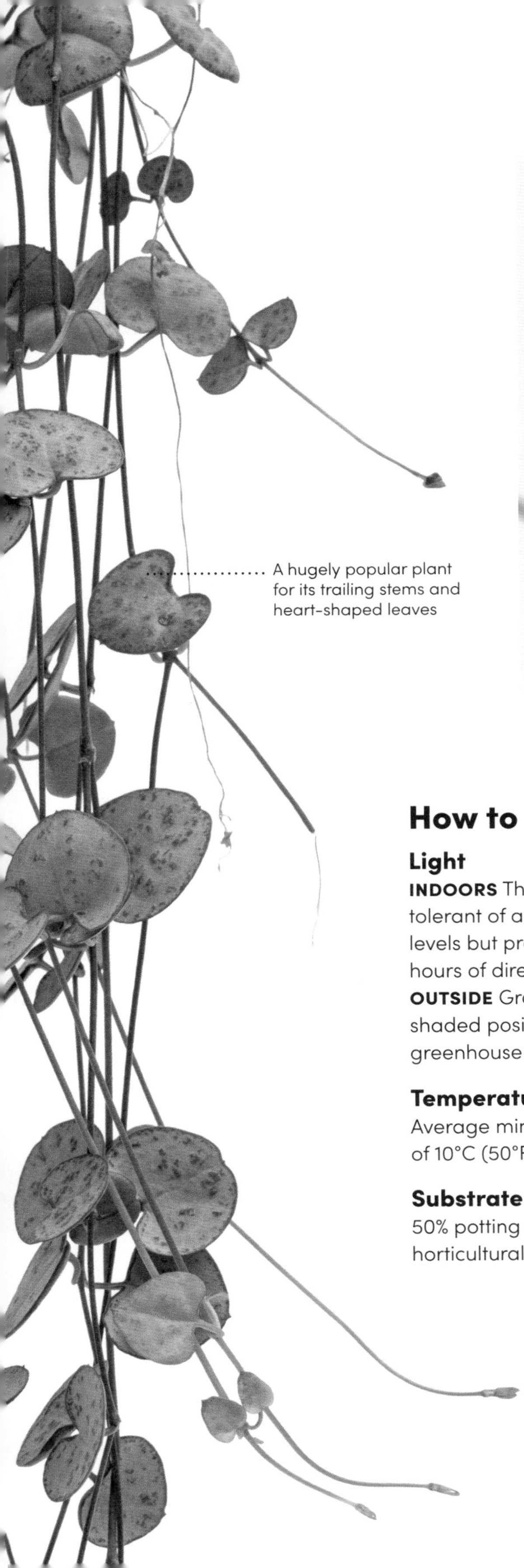

A hugely popular plant for its trailing stems and heart-shaped leaves

Ceropegia sandersonii **flowers are not just pretty; they can trap flies.**

How to grow

Light

INDOORS These plants are tolerant of a wide range of light levels but prefer at least a few hours of direct sunlight.
OUTSIDE Grow in a semi-shaded position in a greenhouse or garden.

Temperature

Average minimum temperature of 10°C (50°F).

Substrate

50% potting compost, 50% horticultural sand/grit/perlite.

Feeding

Once a month during the growing season.

Water

In spring to autumn, water when the substrate has completely dried out. Keep dry in cold temperatures.

RECOMMENDED SPECIES

Ceropegia sandersonii
Grow for the amazing greenish-white, umbrella-like flowers.

C. woodii
Hairy, lilac-pink flowers. Small but fascinating. Try growing across a long, oblong-shaped pot instead of hanging.

C. dichotoma
Unusual thick-stemmed plant with lantern-shaped yellow flowers.

Species have various growth habits, including finger-like stems

Cheiridopsis denticulata

"Bizarre yet beautiful"

Cheiridopsis

Family *Aizoaceae*
Subfamily *Ruschioideae*
Common name Carpet weed, lobster claws

Known for their unique, rubbery, claw-like leaves and vibrant flowers, these resilient clump-forming plants are popular for xeriscaping and rock gardens, creating a carpet of succulent foliage.

The genus *Cheiridopsis* is native to southern Namibia and the Northern and Western Cape Province of South Africa. The name derives from the Greek *cheiris*, meaning "sleeve" or "sheath", which describes the process of the old leaves withering and forming a papery sheath covering the succeeding pair of leaves. The species have pretty daisy-like flowers in a range of colours from white, to yellow, through orange, reds, and purple, which make a delightful burst of colour in the garden. One of my favourites is *C. peculiaris*, which is, as the name suggests, rather peculiar. The plant appears to have two different types of leaves. The lower ones lie flat to the ground, reaching about 5cm (2in), and from within these emerge upright, fuller leaves and flower buds. Depending on the amount of light they get, the leaves can turn the most amazing pinky-purple colour, and look a little bit like a tongue, adding to the bizarre yet beautiful appearance.

RECOMMENDED SPECIES

Cheiridopsis candidissima
Large, greyish, V-shaped leaves with cream to yellow flowers. Leaf tips produce an interesting teeth-like appearance.

C. pillansii
Low-growing with pairs of small, hoof-shaped leaves, pale green to purple in colour. Commonly called the hoof mesemb.

C. denticulata
Yellow flowers, and distinctive foliage with narrow, light-blue, upward-curving leaves, which grow in opposite pairs and with sun exposure turn purple or pink, giving rise to their common name of pink fingers.

How to grow

Light

INDOORS Full, direct sun on the brightest windowsill or in a conservatory.
OUTSIDE Full, direct sunlight, but allow some shade if very hot in summer when most go into dormancy.

Temperature

Average minimum temperature of 5°C (41°F) is recommended for safety, although some species can tolerate lower than this for a short period, provided they are kept bone dry and it warms up during the day.

Substrate

50% potting compost, 50% sand and grit.

Feeding

Once a month during the growing season.

Water

Only water minimally in summer (when they have a resting period) if the plant starts shrivelling. Water more abundantly when they are growing in the autumn and spring. Reduce watering in winter in cold temperatures.

Some species, like *Cheiridopsis vanzylii*, form clumps, each growth consisting of pairs of leaves.

Conophytum

Family *Aizoaceae*
Subfamily *Ruschioideae*
Common name Cone plants, dumplings, button plants, lips plant, conos

---

Conophytum **species are among some of the most pared-back plants in existence, consisting of little more than a pair of fused, juicy leaves that are absorbed and regenerated each year.**

Some species of *Conophytum* are often confused for *Lithops* (see page 224), which is understandable, as they have much in common, including their native habitat of the Western, Northern, and Eastern Cape of South Africa and southern parts of Namibia. *Conophytum* are distinguishable because their leaves are ball-shaped, tubular, conical, cylindrical, or ovate, rather than flattened like *Lithops*. They also tend to be fully fused or have a slight cleft, rather than a full fissure between them. They produce only one pair of leaves at a time, although one plant may have dozens of stems and therefore dozens of leaf pairs, forming a cushion-like cluster. The leaves range from green and blue to red and brown.

These plants produce beautiful daisy-like flowers in a wide range of colours, which can be day-blooming or night-blooming depending on the species. Most of them produce flowers in late summer through to early autumn. *Conophytum* have a spring/summer resting period, when the old leaves shrivel up. It might look like the plant is dying but it is simply protecting the new leaves in a paper sheath until they are fully formed.

"Cute as a button"

The round or cone-shaped leaves often have a partial cleft

Conophytum uviforme

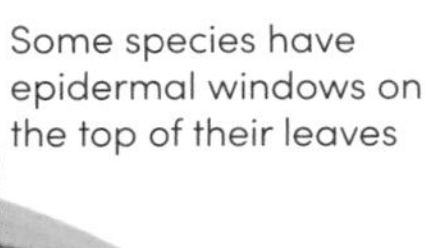

Some species have epidermal windows on the top of their leaves

Conophytum subfenestratum

How to grow

Light

INDOORS Best positioned on the brightest windowsill or in a conservatory.

OUTSIDE Semi-shade is beneficial during hot days in the garden or greenhouse.

Temperature

Average minimum temperature of 5°C (41°F) is recommended for safety, although some species can tolerate lower than this for a short period.

Substrate

50% potting compost, 50% horticultural sand/grit/perlite.

Feeding

Once a month during the growing season.

Water

During the longer, hot days of spring/summer, when they are resting and the old leaves are shrivelling, keep them dry. When plants begin growing in August/September, it is safe to water.

RECOMMENDED SPECIES

Conophytum minutum
Aptly named as this is one of the smallest succulent species. Flowers are pink, purple, or white.

C. uviforme
Grey-green leaves with an intriguing purple veining pattern.

C. taylorianum
Rock-like in appearance. Produces an abundance of flowers late in the summer.

C. minimum
Grey-green leaves speckled or lined with purple/reddish patterning. Lovely scented night-time flowers. Very desirable.

C. pageae
Known as the lips plant because the centre of each pair of leaves, where the flower emerges, has a pinky-red tint resembling lips.

Grower profile

Ferah and Gülen

(@Cactus.Sisters)

Location Melbourne, Australia

Specialism Growing outdoors

Ferah and Gülen are two sisters with a shared passion for growing cacti in their gardens. They enjoy cultivating plants from seed and the beauty of cacti in bloom.

What advice would you give beginners who are thinking of starting their own collection?

The best advice we can give is to grow what you love. Start with cheap, readily available species and learn from growing these. If and when they die, they are easily replaced. Isolate all your new purchases and look to see if they bring a disease or new weed to your garden. *Echinopsis* species, *Lobivia* species, *Notocactus leninghausii, Notocactus magnificus,* and *Echinocereus* are some of the best beginner cacti to grow. They are harder to kill, are small to suit indoors or gardens, and flower beautifully.

What inspired you to create a cacti garden?

In Melbourne, it's rare for temperatures to drop to zero, so the climate conditions are suitable for growing cacti outdoors. I decided to plant some of the tall survivors from my original collection in the ground. Small seedlings of *Trichocereus scopulicola, Pilosocereus azureus,* a grapefruit-size *Echinocactus grusonii,* and a *Myrtillocactus geometrizans* were planted and they grew very well over the years. The *Myrtillocactus* grew like a candelabra to 1.5 metres (5ft).

What were the main considerations when designing the garden?

You need to consider the size and shape of the cacti when mature. You plant the small, globular cacti at the front, medium ones in the middle, and the tall, columnar cacti at the back. Gülen's garden is designed this way. I grouped sections of my garden as smalls, mediums, and talls, trying to reduce tall ones shading the smalls. Any *Echinopsis* and *Trichocereus scopulicola* are great landscaping cacti.

What advice would you give about caring for plants outside?

Cacti will grow beautifully and flower better when grown in sunny positions, in a well-draining medium, with small amounts of fertilizer. During the dry season they may need to be watered. Cacti look plump when well and shrunken when they need watering. Yellowing is an indication that they need a slow-release fertilizer. Cacti can grow in some extreme conditions, but it's a myth that they *have* to grow in these conditions.

What are the biggest challenges you face?

The excessively wet conditions the last two years have resulted in some large cacti getting root rot, but cacti will grow from cuttings, so this year I've been potting up cuttings of the special cacti in case of loss. Some will also be protected in a sheltered area, so they don't get the winter rain.

How do you deal with pests?

Weeding and keeping the cacti healthy is the best form of pest prevention. However, when you have thousands of plants, pests and diseases will happen. Ants and mealybugs need to be controlled. We use an organic insecticide. If a cactus is seriously infected, seal it in a bag and put it in the rubbish; it's not worth saving. It is much harder to control fungal disease; cut and remove infected pieces from your garden. Copper solution is antifungal, and I learnt recently that one part cow's milk, five parts water is also a remedy.

The cacti landscape, from tiny globular plants to towering columns, and everything in between.

***Echinopsis* hybrid 'Vic Market Red' in full flower.**

What has been your greatest success?

Growing from seed is a progression from years of interest in cacti. The first seeds were collected from my garden and sown in January 2019. They were open-pollinated, which means the flowers weren't covered and bees pollinated them from whatever was flowering in the garden at the time. The huge variety of cacti we have in our gardens has resulted in some very interesting open-pollinated progeny. Seeing their first flowers is extremely rewarding – Gülen and I love sending each other first-flower photos. We've been sharing cacti all our lives and the first pups always go to each other.

"The lucky plant"

Crassula ovata

Crassula

Family *Crassulaceae*
Subfamily *Crassuloideae*
Common name Jade plant, money plant

The plump green leaves of the best-known species, *Crassula ovata*, are reminiscent of jade, which symbolizes prosperity and immortality in Chinese culture. This is why many Chinese shops and restaurants have large species growing in the window.

Native to southern Africa, *Crassula* is a large genus of approximately 200 to 300 species, but only a small percentage are popular in cultivation, since many need space to sprawl.

C. ovata – the jade or money plant – can be very long-lived. My local Chinese takeaway has an enormous 75-year-old plant that produces beautiful small, white, star-shaped flowers in the late winter to early spring. The most commonly grown *Crassula*, however, remain relatively small and compact, and flower in the winter months when many other plants are dormant.

How to grow

Light

INDOORS The compact growth seen in their habitat requires high light levels, preferably direct sunlight, for at least part of the day.
OUTSIDE A semi-shaded position in a greenhouse or garden.

Temperature

Average minimum temperature of 5°C (41°F) is recommended for safety, although some species can tolerate lower for a short period if kept dry.

Substrate

50% potting compost, 50% horticultural sand/grit/perlite.

Feeding

Once or twice during the growing season.

Water

In spring to autumn water when the substrate has completely dried out. Keep dry in cold temperatures and only water if the leaves appear to shrink or shrivel.

RECOMMENDED SPECIES

Crassula ovata
Resembling a chunky, shrunken tree, this is one of my all-time favourite succulents. Old specimens are awe-inspiring. No home should be without one.

***C.* 'Buddha's Temple'**
Densely stacked greyish-green leaves form a bizarre square column up to 15cm (6in) tall. Easily killed from too much water and a lack of light.

C. plegmatoides
An extraordinary plant with greyish rounded leaves closely clasping one another, stacked together in upright columns. Mature specimens bend and twist, creating unruly madness.

C. muscosa
Composed of tiny, densely packed green leaves that overlap in a scale-like pattern.

Curio

Family *Asteraceae*
Subfamily *Asteroideae*
Common name String of pearls, string of dolphins, string of bananas

Sold as a hanging plant, this ground creeper would feel more at home scrambling over a rocky area in the garden or sprawling across a large shallow dish where the stems can grow horizontally rather than vertically.

Curio, formerly included in the genus *Senecio*, exhibits a wide array of forms, including those with bead-, banana-, finger-, and dolphin-like fleshy leaves in colours ranging from deep green to blue-green. In its natural habitat of South Africa, *C. rowleyanus*, better known as string of pearls, sprawls across the ground, rooting wherever it touches the soil, forming a dense mat. Unlike cacti and many other succulent plants, it stores water not in its stem but in its ball-shaped leaves. The round "pearls" minimize water loss while maximizing water storage potential at the same time.

Growing *Curio* as nature intended, rather than as a hanging houseplant, prevents the thin stems from snapping under the weight of the leaves. The genus belongs to the same family as dandelions, daisies, and ragworts, so perhaps it is not surprising that these plants produce small, daisy-like flowers, which typically appear in the autumn or early winter.

"Curio by name, curio by nature"

Curio rowleyanus

Though a ground creeper, *Curio* is often sold as a hanging plant

How to grow

Light

INDOORS Grow on a south-, east-, or west-facing windowsill or in a conservatory.
OUTSIDE A semi-shaded position in a greenhouse or garden.

Temperature

Average minimum temperature of 5°C (41°F) is recommended for safety, although some species can tolerate lower for a short period if kept dry.

Substrate

Often the substrate *Curio* is sold in is too water-retentive, so it's advisable to repot into a mix of 50% potting compost, 50% horticultural sand/grit/perlite.

Feeding

Once a month during the growing season.

Water

In spring to autumn water when the substrate has completely dried out. Water less frequently during winter.

RECOMMENDED SPECIES

***Curio rowleyanus* 'Variegata'**
Has spherical leaves with green, cream, and pink variegation.

C. herreanus
The curiously shaped and patterned leaves resemble the skin of a watermelon.

C. radicans
Has tendrils of glossy, banana-shaped foliage.

C. repens
A semi-trailing, low-growing dwarf shrub with silvery-blue, finger-like, fleshy leaves.

The pearl-shaped, succulent leaves have evolved to store water.

Dioscorea

Family *Dioscoreaceae*
Subfamily *Dioscoreoideae*
Common name Yam, elephant's foot

Commonly known as yam, *Dioscorea* is a genus with a rich history. Several species are grown as agricultural crops for their underground tubers, while others have been used for arrow poison, fishing bait, and even birth control.

Dioscorea is a genus of over 600 species, spread throughout the tropics and subtropics. They have tuberous roots, or caudices (specialized swollen stem bases), a vining growth habit, and small, yellow-green flowers. Perhaps the most interesting species is *D. mexicana*, which was discovered to contain the steroid precursor diosgenin, which was used in progesterone production and made the contraceptive pill more affordable and widely available.

The caudex is the food- and water-storing organ and has a thick, woody exterior to protect it from being eaten by animals. In some cases these caudices can grow as much as 3 metres (10ft) in height. Caudiciforms separate jobs between their caudex and leaves: the former stores the water; the latter conduct photosynthesis. Like many desert plants they have a dormancy period, when the leaves drop, so for some months of the year all that remains is the caudex, which can look like little more than a potato in a pot. For collectors, *D. elephantipes* is one of the most coveted for its deeply fissured caudex, which gives rise to the common name elephant's foot.

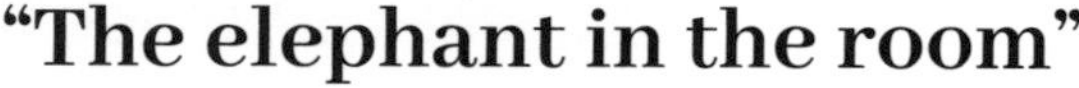

Dioscorea elephantipes

It can be helpful to use a support for the stems of *Dioscorea elephantipes* to climb.

How to grow

Light

INDOORS Needs direct sunlight when growing, on the brightest windowsill or in a conservatory. **OUTSIDE** The leaves like direct sunlight but the caudex prefers to be shaded. When the plant is dormant, make sure the caudex isn't in direct sunlight.

Temperature

Average minimum temperature of 5°C (41°F) is recommended for safety, although some species can tolerate lower for a short period if kept dry.

Substrate

80% grit/sand/pumice,
20% potting compost.

Feeding

Only when growing (i.e. when there are leaves on the plant).

Water

When growing, they tend to need a lot of water. Check the substrate regularly during the growing season and water as soon as it becomes dry. Try not to get water on the caudex to reduce the risk of rot. Don't water when dormant. As a rule: NO vine = NO water.

The woody caudex can be extremely tough, to protect it from animals

---

RECOMMENDED SPECIES

Dioscorea elephantipes
The leaves are small and shallowly heart-shaped, but the star of the show is the incredible caudex, which resembles a turtle shell or elephant's foot. Old specimens are a sight to behold.

D. sylvatica
Also known as forest elephant's foot. As young plants they have a smooth, almost conical caudex, which becomes wrinkled and then fissured as they age.

Dracaena

Family *Asparagaceae*
Subfamily *Nolinoideae*
Common name Dragon tree, snake plant

Surprisingly few books on succulents mention *Dracaena*, and yet the snake plant (*D. trifasciata*), known for its serpentine, sword-like leaves, is one of the most common succulents grown as a houseplant.

Dracaena is a genus of about 120 species of trees and succulent shrubs, the majority of which are native to Africa and southern Asia through to northern Australia. Species can be separated into two growth types: tree-like, which have above-ground stems, and rhizomatous, such as *D. angolensis* (syn. *Sansevieria cylindrica*), which have underground rhizomes – horizontal stems, which put out lateral shoots and adventitious roots, making them easy to propagate by simply cutting them in two.

The largest species in the genus is *D. draco*, also known as dragon tree, a stunning evergreen succulent tree with bluish foliage, which would make a unique and striking addition to any warm garden. Many of the smaller species make great houseplants. They are some of the easiest to care for as long as they are planted in free-draining substrate, get good light, and are not overwatered.

"A favourite house guest"

Dracaena masoniana

Dracaena leaves can adapt to a wide variety of light conditions

How to grow

Light

INDOORS Many species are better able to adapt to lower light conditions than other succulent plants, but that's not to say you should deny them bright light. They do best grown close to a bright window or in a conservatory.
OUTSIDE Partial shade or dappled sun in the garden or greenhouse.

Temperature

Average minimum temperature of 10°C (50°F) is recommended for safety, although some species can tolerate lower than this.

Substrate

50% potting compost, 50% sand/grit/pumice/perlite.

Feeding

Once or twice a year in the growing season.

Water

Allow the substrate to completely dry out before watering. Keep dry in the cold winter months.

RECOMMENDED SPECIES

***Dracaena pethera* var. *pulchra* 'Coppertone' (formerly *Sansevieria kirkii* 'Coppertone')**
Has thick, sculptural leaves and, as the name suggests, is the most wonderful copper colour. Easy to propagate via rhizome cutting.

D. francisii
Leaves are elongated, pointed, and spirally arranged, growing upwards in compact rows until the plant bends under its own weight and sends out stolons, from which more leaves grow. They are slow-growing, so try to find a big specimen to buy.

D. masoniana
Often grown as a single large leaf; it will produce others, but slowly. Buy a few single leaves and plant them together for a striking display. The common name is whale fin or shark's fin due to the fin-shaped leaves.

Echeveria

Family *Crassulaceae*
Subfamily *Sempervivoideae*
Common name Hen and chicks, Mexican rose, Mexican gem

If there were ever a geometrically perfect plant, this would be it. Looking more like flowers than plants, the rosettes of these "stonecrops" vary in colour, ranging from blue-green to pink, purple, and red.

Typically found growing on rocky outcrops, *Echeveria* make such popular houseplants because of their compact size and minimal care requirements. The species are known as polycarpic, meaning that they may flower and set seed many times over the course of their lifetimes. Often, these plants will produce numerous offsets, which gives rise to the common name hen and chicks (which can also refer to other genera such as *Sempervivum*).

There are two distinctive forms: low-growing and small shrubs, which produce rosettes on longer stems. Grown outside, the rosettes remain compact and vibrantly coloured; inside, they can become a little leggy if not given enough light. In ideal conditions plants produce tall flower spikes with pretty, long-lasting, bell-shaped flowers in hues of yellow, orange, and red. Rosettes can grow upwards of 60cm (24in) in diameter.

Bell-like flowers in bright colours rise on tall stalks from fleshy rosettes

"Stone roses"

Echeveria secunda* var. *glauca

How to grow

Light

INDOORS On a bright windowsill or in a conservatory that receives direct sunlight for at least 4 to 5 hours.
OUTSIDE Grow in full sun or partial shade in a garden or greenhouse.

Temperature

Average minimum temperature of 5°C (41°F) is recommended for safety, although some species can tolerate lower than this for a short period if kept dry.

Substrate

50% potting compost,
50% horticultural sand/grit.

Feeding

Once a month during the growing season.

Water

Allow the substrate to dry out between waterings. If you have cold winters, don't water at all during this season unless leaves are shrivelling. If the rosette covers the pot, sit it in water to saturate from below.

Echeveria **'Duchess of Nuremberg' has a stunning pinky-purple flush to its leaves and flowers.**

RECOMMENDED SPECIES

Echeveria cante
Also known as white cloud plant because of the powder-coated, silvery-blue leaves, often with a red-tinged edge along the margins. Simply beautiful.

***E. runyonii* 'Topsy Turvy'**
A spectacular form, which has very unusual curled leaves.

E. derenbergii
Also known as the painted-lady, this plant rapidly produces a colony of small offsets perfect for gifting to friends and family.

E. elegans
Intense sunlight tinges the tips of the soft-blue leaves with pink. The flower stems are candy-pink with contrasting vibrant yellow flowers. A very popular clump species.

E. subrigida
Bright-green leaves edged with red. The rosettes can grow to 60cm (24in) in diameter and just as high over time. The plant takes on a very striking appearance outside in full sun.

Euphorbia

Family *Euphorbiaceae*
Subfamily *Euphorbioideae*
Common name Spurge

There are thousands of species of *Euphorbia*, many of which are completely bizarre-looking, which is why I'm so fond of this genus. Most are also easy to grow, and make excellent houseplants.

Euphorbia is a very big, very diverse genus of plants, commonly called spurge. This name derives from the Middle English/Old French word espurge ("to purge"), due to the use of the plant's sap as a purgative.

Succulent euphorbias are from arid regions of southern Africa and Madagascar, but not all species are succulent. Those that are have evolved characteristics similar to cacti, which they are often mistaken for (for more on convergent evolution see page 11). Some are thorny, fleshy shrubs, some are globular, while others are columnar with ribs and branches. What they all have in common is a latex-like sap, which is an irritant and poisonous, so care must be taken when propagating. A useful tip to stop the flow of sap is to submerge the cut stem in water.

"Handle with care"

Euphorbia ingens

How to grow

Light

INDOORS Best suited to a south-, east-, or west-facing windowsill or conservatory.
OUTSIDE Full sun or semi-shade in a garden or greenhouse.

Temperature

Average minimum temperature of 5°C (41°F) is recommended for safety, although some species can tolerate lower.

Substrate

50% potting compost, 50% sand/grit/pumice/perlite.

Feeding

Once or twice a year in the spring/summer growing season.

Water

Allow the substrate to completely dry out before watering. Keep dry in the cold winter months.

Some species of *Euphorbia* look strikingly like cacti

The thickly ribbed *Euphorbia horrida*, also known as African milk barrel, in flower.

RECOMMENDED SPECIES

Euphorbia caput-medusae
Resembles the head of Medusa, with snake-like stems growing from a central caudex.

E. platyclada
Also known as the dead plant because it looks like a bunch of dead sticks, though up close it has the most beautiful mottled stems, which take on a pinky colour in bright sunlight.

E. obesa
Aka the baseball plant, this is a smooth, spherical-to-columnar solitary plant with subtle "zipper-like" patterns down the sides.

E. horrida
Fairly slow-growing but produces prolific offsets. When mature the stems often grow prostrate. There is a particularly lovely cultivar, 'Snowflake', with whitish stems.

E. bupleurifolia
Known as cycad spurge or pine cone plant because the caudiciform trunk looks like a small pine cone topped with a crown of green leaves.

Faucaria tigrine

The thick wedge-shaped leaves are edged with soft teeth

Faucaria

Family *Aizoaceae*
Subfamily *Ruschioideae*
Common name Tiger jaws, shark jaws, cat jaws

"Word of mouth"

The name *Faucaria* is derived from the Latin word for "animal throat", and it's very apt for this genus. The paired, toothed leaves bear a striking resemblance to the gaping jaws of a tiger.

Faucaria is a genus of around eight species, native to the Cape Province of South Africa and the Karoo Desert, with most found growing among rocks. The plants belonging to this genus are characterized by fleshy triangular leaves with rows of "teeth" that curve inwards along the margin. Some species are mottled, furrowed, or adorned with calcium oxalate crystal concentrations, usually visible as small dots.

The angular rosettes form clumps and produce daisy-like yellow or white flowers in autumn, which appear from between the topmost leaves, opening during the late afternoon and closing at sunset. *Faucaria* won't bloom if they don't get at least three to four hours of direct sun and are more than a few years old. The rosettes will produce offsets, which grow into quite a substantial clump over time. These plants are a good choice for outdoor ground cover in a rockery as they are quite hardy and some species can take a short period of light frost. Propagation is best done by seed, as leaf cuttings can be difficult to root.

RECOMMENDED SPECIES

Faucaria tigrina
Distinctly flecked leaves with many teeth, resembling alligator jaws. In the garden they offset in a circular growth habit, making a unique and attractive carpet of ground cover.

***F. tuberculosa* cv. 'Super Warty'**
A monstrous cultivar with large, warty growths on the leaf. Also bears white, soft teeth along the margins. Spectacularly odd.

F. britteniae
One of the hardiest species. It can handle very light frost if kept dry.

How to grow

Light

INDOORS Full, direct sun on the brightest windowsill or in a conservatory. As houseplants they tend to grow in warm, sunny weather and rest when it's too hot or too cool.
OUTSIDE Full, direct sunlight in a garden or greenhouse.

Temperature

Average minimum temperature of 5°C (41°F) is recommended for safety, although some species are frost-hardy and can tolerate much lower than this if kept dry.

Substrate

50% potting mix, 50% grit/pumice/perlite.

Feeding

Once a month during the growing season.

Water

Allow to completely dry out between waterings. Withhold water in cold temperatures.

Grower profile

Lyn Kimberley

Location Belfast, Northern Ireland

Specialism Cacti and succulent horticulturist

Membership British Cactus and Succulent Society

With over 42 years' experience, Lyn's impressive collection of around 2,000 cacti and succulents thrives in a large polytunnel. Her love for these plants led her to launch her YouTube channel, Desert Plants of Avalon, in 2012, where she shares her knowledge with a growing audience of fellow enthusiasts.

When did you first become interested in cacti and succulents?

When I was 11 years old, my big brother Mike came home with some plants he had bought from a local garden centre. They were a *Chamaecereus silvestrii, Polaskia chichipe, Opuntia microdasys,* and a *Haworthia,* and I was fascinated – so much so that he ended up giving them to me. It was a love affair with cacti and succulents from that day on.

If you could only keep three plants from your collection, which would they be?

1. My *Rebutia albipilosa*. It's one I have grown for over 25 years and it produces the most gorgeous orange blooms in spring and summer.

2. My *Parodia magnifica*. It's one of my favourite specimens. This cactus never fails to give me the most beautiful display of bright-yellow blooms. I also love how it produces so many pups around its base.

3. My triple-headed *Ferocactus*, which I have grown for almost 30 years. It got top rot many years ago and I had to slice the top off the crown, but over time it recovered and has grown three big, amazing top heads with fierce-looking red spines.

How do you deal with pests?

I use horticultural neem oil mixed with horticultural soap to treat and prevent pests like mealybugs and red spider mites. I use it as a spray and also as a soil drench every month from spring until late summer. I also spray and dab isopropyl alcohol onto any pests I see; this works well in winter, when I need to keep the plants dry, as it dries fast. I also brush diatomaceous earth onto my plants with a big powder brush, which helps keep pests at bay.

What advice would you give about watering through the seasons?

Keep most cacti and succulents dry over the winter months, as this is when they have their rest period. Watering arid cacti in winter can cause them to rot, as they are not in active growth, but from April until mid-September I would water them every time the soil has dried out. The exception would be the epiphytic cacti, such as *Schlumbergera* and *Rhipsalis;* they still need to be lightly watered during winter.

Five of the best beginner plants?

1. ***Echinopsis subdenudata.*** These cacti are easy to grow and will produce amazing big white flowers. They will grow well on a sunny windowsill.

2. ***Mammillaria.*** This large genus of cacti is very easy blooming and easy to grow.

3. ***Parodia.*** Also amazing bloomers, easy to grow, and readily available.

4. ***Rhipsalis.*** These cacti are epiphytic and grow very well indoors, as they don't need the high sunlight that arid cacti need. They are perfect plants to grow in bathrooms, as they love humidity.

5. ***Echeveria.*** These beautiful rosette succulents can be pruned and propagated so easily from leaves and stems.

Lyn's 25-year-old *Parodia magnifica* (top) and *Schlumbergera truncata* (above) in bloom.

What are your top tips for plant care?

My top tips would be to research the plants as much as possible. Some need less light or more water, and some can take the cold in winter and some cannot. Repot them into a container no more than a little bigger than the last, and make sure you use a very well-draining soil mix – cacti and succulents won't grow well in traditional houseplant soil. Treat and isolate any plants with pests as soon as you see them.

Gasteria

Family *Asphodelaceae*
Subfamily *Asphodeloideae*
Common name Ox-tongue, cow-tongue, lawyer's tongue

Gasteria **make excellent houseplants, tolerating less light than many other succulents. The pretty flowers are edible and a traditional component of stews.**

Gasteria species are similar to *Aloe* except their leaves are "two-ranked", or distichous, meaning they are arranged alternately in two vertical columns on opposite sides of the stem. Most *Gasteria* are native to the Eastern Cape Province, South Africa, with some species extending into the far southwest corner of Namibia. How many species belong to the genus is inconclusive (but currently thought to be under 20), as differentiating between them can be extremely difficult. A plant can look very different depending on its location, the substrate in which it grows, and its age. Hybrids also occur easily in their natural habitat. Usually, young plants have flat, strappy, tongue-like leaves but often look different when mature. Leaf colours range from very dark green through to greys and are usually mottled but can also be striped or solid colours.

"Tasty on the tongue"

Gasteria carinata

How to grow

Light

INDOORS A bright windowsill, which receives a few hours of direct sunlight in the morning.
OUTSIDE A semi-shaded position. In a greenhouse, provide some shading. Too much sun will turn leaves red or dull their colour.

Temperature

Average minimum temperature of 10°C (50°F) is recommended for safety, although some species can tolerate lower than this for a short period.

Substrate

50% potting compost, 50% horticultural sand/grit/perlite.

Feeding

Once a month during the growing season.

Water

From spring to autumn water when the substrate has completely dried out. If temperatures drop during winter, water less frequently.

RECOMMENDED SPECIES

Gasteria obtusa
Produces lots of offsets, with spotted grey/green leaves. Forms a large attractive clump of fan-like plants.

G. batesiana
A smallish species with very rough, dagger-shaped leaves that form a rosette in a mature plant. The bands of mottling give the leaves a striped look.

G. carinata
A highly variable species. Typically, it has thick, sharp, triangular leaves, with tiny spots arranged in bands, giving them faint stripes.

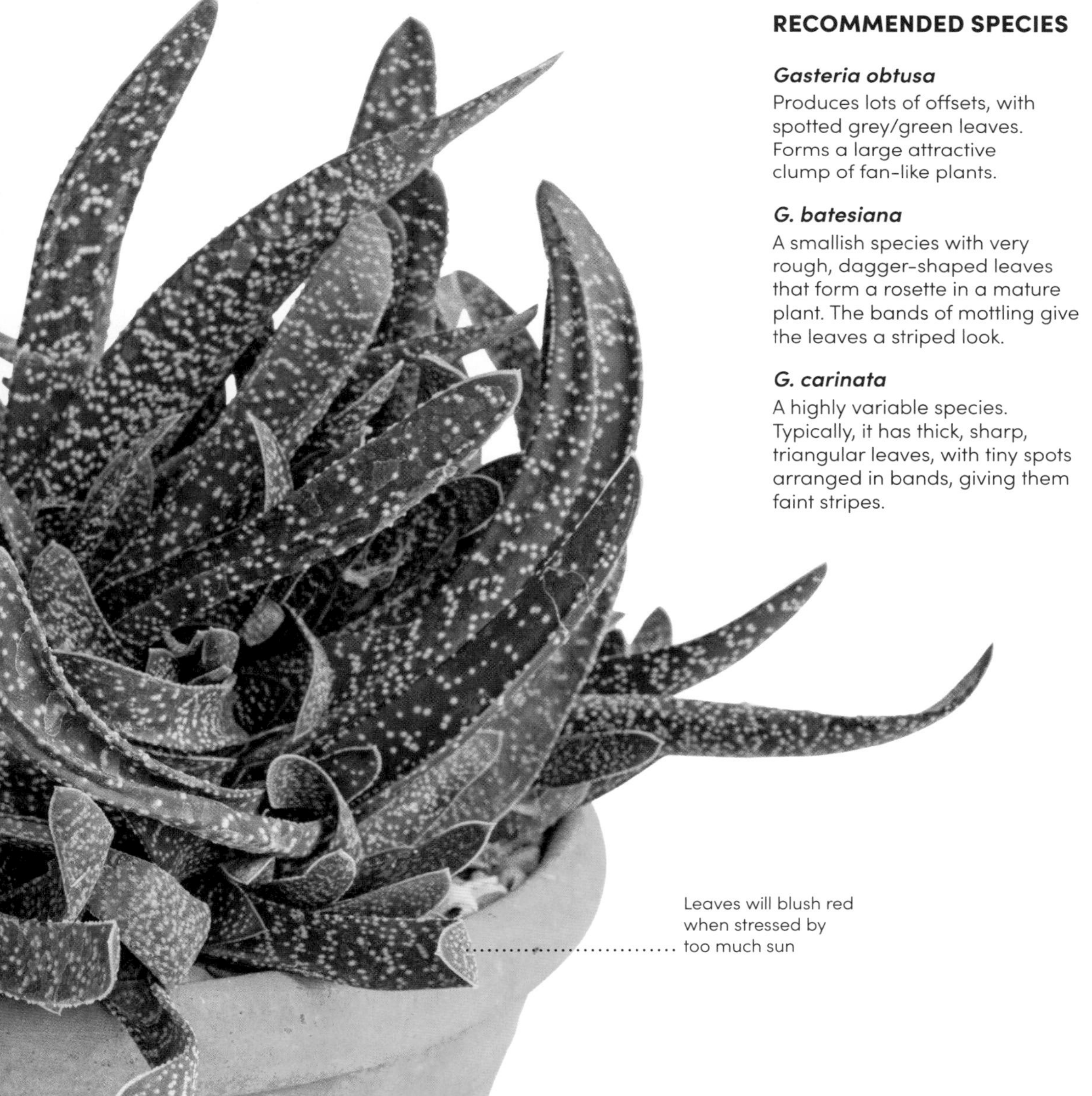

Leaves will blush red when stressed by too much sun

Graptopetalum

Family *Crassulaceae*
Subfamily *Sempervivoideae*
Common name Leatherpetal, ghost plant, mother of pearl plant

This versatile succulent makes an excellent houseplant, unusual ground cover, or a container plant. The name, from the Greek *graptos*, meaning "inscribed, marked, or painted", describes the markings on the flower petals of many species.

Closely related to *Echeveria* (see page 204) and *Sedum* (see page 238), *Graptopetalum* is a genus of less than 20 species native to Mexico and Arizona. Blooming in spring, they produce dainty star-shaped whitish, yellow, red, or orange flowers, many with red-brown dots or tiny lines on the topsides of the inner lower parts of each petal. The leaves are thick and break off easily when touched, so take care when moving or repotting them. The upside is that any fallen leaves can be easily propagated by simply laying them on top of the soil, where they will sprout roots and tiny leaves.

The leaves are pale, giving plants a ghostly appearance, but the appeal of *Graptopetalum* is the diversity of colours, ranging from pastel greens through blue, pinks, purples, yellows, and orange, which change depending on the light intensity. The leaves form elegant rosettes, some at the end of sprawling, ever-lengthening stems that become pendant over time. Combining a few species together is a great way to add a pop of colour to the garden. In cold regions, plant into a pot that can be moved inside during winter.

"A ghostly vision"

Graptopetalum filiferum

How to grow

Light

INDOORS On a bright windowsill or in a conservatory that receives direct sunlight for at least a few hours.
OUTSIDE Full sun or partial shade in a garden or greenhouse.

Leaves are often a pale grey-green but can be tinged with pink

Temperature

Average minimum temperature of 5°C (41°F) is recommended for safety, although some species can tolerate lower than 0°C (32°F) for a short period if kept dry.

Substrate

50% potting compost, 50% horticultural sand/grit.

Feeding

Once a month during the growing season.

Water

Allow the substrate to completely dry out between waterings. If you experience cold winters, don't water at all during this season unless the leaves start shrivelling.

RECOMMENDED SPECIES

Graptopetalum paraguayense
A cold-hardy succulent with pale-grey or whitish leaves known as ghost plant. It has a creeping habit, which makes interesting groundcover, or it cascades down from a hanging planter.

G. bellum
Clump-forming with lovely pinky-red flowers. Makes a great houseplant.

G. amethystinum
Dusty-lavender, pebble-shaped leaves with an attractive display of bright red-and-yellow flowers.

Haworthia

Family *Asphodelaceae*
Subfamily *Asphodeloideae*
Common name Zebra plant, pearl plant, star window plant, cushion aloe, cut window plant, horse's teeth

---

***Haworthia* species are not grown for their flowers but for their amazing leaf forms, some of which have jewel-like "windows" through which sunlight can reach their internal photosynthetic tissues.**

Haworthia are a great choice for indoor gardeners owing to their compact size, tolerance of lower light than many other succulents, and fascinating growth habit. Many remain as single rosettes, while others form clumps. The smallest and one of the rarest, *H. parksiana*, is just 3cm (1¼in) in diameter, while others can be up to 30cm (12in). The inflorescences, although not particularly noteworthy, can exceed 40cm (15¾in) in height. Most species are native to South Africa, but some are found in Eswatini (formerly Swaziland), southern Namibia, and southern Mozambique, where they grow mainly in savannahs, grasslands, and thickets, in the shade of rocks or other plants. Sometimes the leaves will turn an attractive red or orangey colour in hot weather but regain their usual green colour in cooler temperatures. The actual number of the species within the genus is difficult to know because of the difficulties of *Haworthia* taxonomy, which includes many varieties.

"The jewels of the succulent world"

***Haworthia pumila* cv. 'Angel's Tears'**

Haworthia truncata has translucent leaf windows to aid photosynthesis.

How to grow

Light

INDOORS Grow on a bright windowsill, which receives a few hours of direct sunlight.
OUTSIDE Grow in a semi-shaded position. In a greenhouse, provide some shading.

Temperature

Average minimum temperature of 5°C (41°F) is recommended for safety, although some species can tolerate lower than this for a short period if kept dry.

Substrate

50% potting compost, 50% horticultural sand/grit/perlite.

Feeding

Once a month during the growing season.

Water

In spring to autumn water when the substrate has completely dried out. If temperatures drop during winter, water less frequently.

Often forms compact rosettes, but flower stalks can be very tall

RECOMMENDED SPECIES

Haworthia coarctata* var. *adelaidensis
A clump-forming plant with narrow, extended leaves, which form elongated triangular shapes. The leaf surface is densely covered with tiny white spots. In hot weather the green leaves turn the most beautiful deep red.

H. truncata
One of the most fascinating-looking succulents. Fat, oblong leaves with opaque windows, which resemble horses' teeth.

H. cooperi
Usually green but sometimes blueish-purple fleshy leaves with translucent, glass-like windows.

Hoodia

Family *Apocynaceae*
Subfamily *Asclepiadoideae*
Common name Bushman's hat

Hoodia **are deceptive in appearance and can be easily confused for cacti, as they have a similar form, with rows of small thorns visible along the green-brown to green-grey stems.**

The genus *Hoodia* ranges from the western part of southern Africa to central Namibia, and as far north as southern Angola, where it typically grows on rocky slopes and open stone plains. The plant blooms in August or September with a multitude of gorgeous yet bizarre disc-shaped flowers that almost entirely cover the stem, coupled with an unfortunate smell that resembles decaying flesh to attract flies for pollination – but don't let that put you off. *Hoodia* are one of my favourite succulents for their unique appearance and adaptability. Tolerant of less light than some other succulent plants, they make a good indoor plant, although they might be reluctant to flower – which, in this case, might not be a bad thing because of the smell.

"Hoodwinked"

Hoodia gordonii

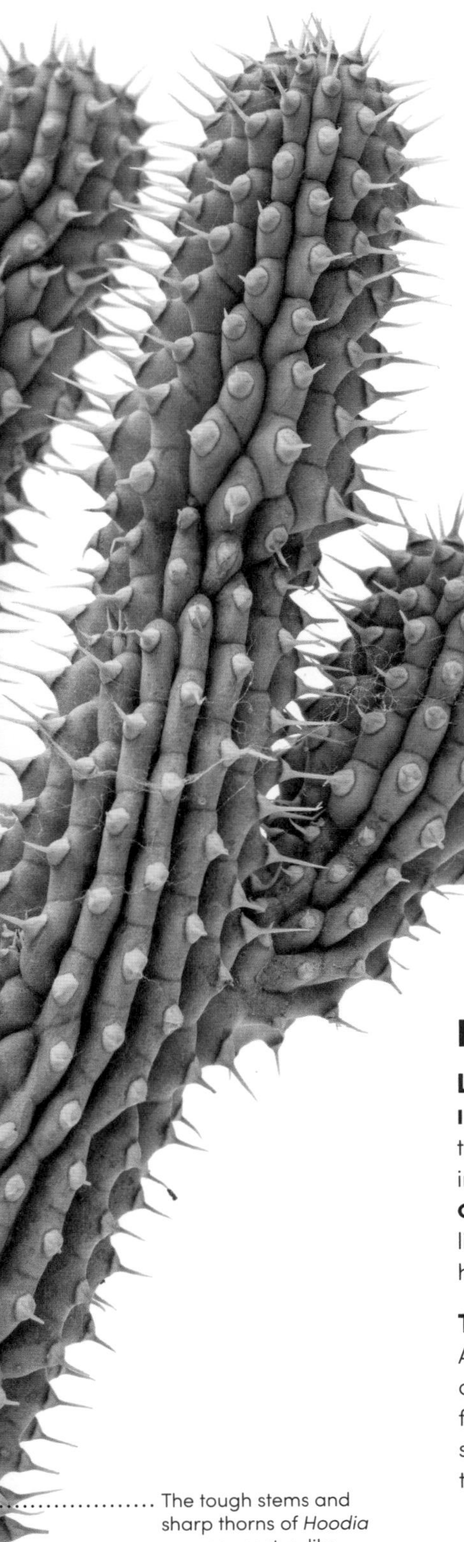

The tough stems and sharp thorns of *Hoodia* are very cactus-like

Hoodia flowers are both bizarre-looking and foul-smelling.

How to grow

Light

INDOORS Best positioned on the brightest windowsill or in a conservatory.
OUTSIDE Will benefit from light shade during the hottest summer days.

Temperature

Average minimum temperature of 5°C (41°F) is recommended for safety, although some species can tolerate lower than this for a short period if kept dry.

Substrate

50% potting compost,
50% horticultural sand/grit.

Feeding

Once or twice during the growing season.

Water

Water when the substrate has totally dried out. Keep dry in the cold winter months.

RECOMMENDED SPECIES

Hoodia gordonii
Blue-green branching stems with flesh-coloured flowers. A stunning combination.

H. currorii
Grey-green stems bear large rust-red flowers with purple hairs.

Huernia

Family *Apocynaceae*
Subfamily *Asclepiadoideae*
Common name Lifesaver plant

What makes this genus so special is its incredibly odd yet captivating flowers. The small, five-pointed blooms are a true marvel of nature, often resembling lifebuoys due to their glossy raised central annulus.

The *Huernia* genus comprises 52 species, widely distributed in sub-Saharan Africa, from Nigeria to South Africa and the Horn of Africa. There are also a handful of species found in the Arabian Peninsula. *Huernia* have some of the most extraordinary flowers in the plant kingdom. They exude a subtle to strong scent, which can range from sweetly aromatic to musty, attracting a variety of pollinators, including flies. Their colour palette is equally diverse, with some species boasting flowers in deep reds, yellows, or oranges, often with fantastical patterns. The angular stems are occasionally speckled with red or purple hues and are often found sprawling across the ground or climbing over rocks, forming dense clusters. *Huernia* are closely related to *Stapelia* (see page 242), which have similarly incredible flowers but are even smellier.

"Circle of life"

Huernia piersii

Thick, fleshy, angular stems often grow in dense clumps

How to grow

Light

INDOORS A bright windowsill, which receives a few hours of direct sunlight in the morning.
OUTSIDE Make sure the plant is shaded during the harsh afternoon sun. In a greenhouse, provide some shading.

Temperature

In winter, best kept in temperatures no lower than about 8–10°C (46–50°F). If it is not possible to provide this temperature in a greenhouse, the plants can be brought inside for the winter and placed near a window.

Substrate

50% potting compost, 50% horticultural sand/grit. A layer of grit on the soil surface prevents moisture from accumulating around the base of the stems.

Feeding

Once a month during the growing season.

Water

If you experience cold winters, don't water at all during this season. At all other times, allow the plant to completely dry out between waterings.

RECOMMENDED SPECIES

Huernia zebrina
One of the most beautiful and popular in cultivation. The star-like, intensely coloured yellow-and-red striped blooms are jaw-dropping.

H. thuretii
Awe-inspiring flowers from pure yellow to leopard-spotted.

H. macrocarpa
Forms clumps of branching, trailing stems and vibrantly coloured flowers in hues of red or purple, with intricate markings. Flowers are sweetly fragranced.

Kalanchoe

Family *Crassulaceae*
Subfamily *Kalanchoideae*
Common name Flaming Katy, chandelier plant, devil's backbone, mother of millions, mother of thousands, velvet elephant ear, felt bush

Many have leaves with scalloped edges and bell flowers on long stalks

Kalanchoe fedtschenkoi

"Buy one get 100 free"

If you are looking for value for money, look no further. *Kalanchoe* is often referred to as mother of thousands or millions because some species can produce an amazing number of plantlets on the leaf margins or inflorescence.

Most *Kalanchoe* are native to Madagascar and tropical Africa, but one species has even been grown in space. In 1971 a small, square, transparent box was attached to a wall of the Salyut 1 space station and plants put inside as an experiment to see what could be grown. The plants were cared for by the astronauts, and although not intended as a morale booster, scientists were so impressed by the positive psychological effect this had on the crew that in 1979, when astronauts complained of struggling with loneliness and depression, a mature *Kalanchoe* plant was sent to the station via a resupply vehicle. The crew named it "life tree" and made sure it was always in the picture during television broadcasts from the station.

There is a great diversity of species within the genus. The largest, *K. beharensis*, can reach 6 metres (19¾ft) tall, but most species are less than 1 metre (3¼ft) tall, many of which make great houseplants for their tolerance to drought and willingness to flower. Note that due to their ability to rapidly reproduce, some species are invasive in non-native countries. Always do your research before planting a *Kalanchoe* outside.

How to grow

Light

INDOORS Best suited to a south-, east-, or west-facing windowsill or conservatory.
OUTSIDE Full sun or semi-shade in a garden or greenhouse.

Temperature

Average minimum temperature of 10°C (50°F) is recommended for safety, although some species can tolerate lower than this for a short period if kept dry.

Substrate

50% potting compost,
50% sand/grit/pumice/perlite.

Feeding

Once or twice a year in the spring and summer growing season.

Water

Allow the substrate to completely dry out before watering. Keep dry in the cold winter months.

***Kalanchoe tomentosa* has furry leaves tinged with brown edges.**

RECOMMENDED SPECIES

Kalanchoe pinnata
Commonly known as cathedral bells because of the large, bell-shaped flowers.

K. beharensis
Large triangular leaves, pale silvery-green in colour, and covered in dense, felt-like hairs. Very strokable.

K. luciae
Often mislabelled as *K. thyrsiflora*, which is very rare in cultivation. Nicknamed paddle plant, desert cabbage, or dog tongue, owing to its rosettes of fleshy leaves with red-tinged edges.

Lithops **(mix)**

Lithops

Family *Aizoaceae*
Subfamily *Ruschioideae*
Common name Living stones, split rocks

"Stony-faced and cheeky"

These peculiar-looking plants have a pair of succulent leaves resembling pebbles or buttocks, depending on how you look at them.

Lithops are found in very dry areas of South Africa but are difficult to spot because of their clever camouflage, mimicking the stones around them to protect themselves from predators. In habitat, the leaves grow almost submerged in the ground, with a translucent surface that acts as a "window", allowing sunlight in for photosynthesis.

To grow, they develop new leaves beneath the old, which split open, like a snake shedding its skin, revealing the fresh, plump leaves beneath. The old leaves eventually shrivel, becoming paper-like and satisfying to peel off. Late summer to early autumn is the time to fully appreciate these bizarre entities when from the fissured centre grow large, daisy-like flowers, which can entirely obscure the plant beneath. Despite their ingenious disguise, they haven't managed to outwit the poachers and, sadly, are on the endangered list.

How to grow

Light

INDOORS Best suited to an area with at least 5 hours of direct sunlight daily. Ideally, the brightest windowsill or a conservatory.

OUTSIDE In an unshaded position in a greenhouse or planted in pots outside, which can be moved inside during poor weather.

Temperature

Average minimum temperature of 5°C (41°F).

Substrate

75% horticultural sand/grit, 25% potting compost.

Feeding

Not necessary, but feeding them once or twice a year with a very diluted, low-nitrogen cactus fertilizer is acceptable.

Water

They go dormant in summer, so water should be restricted during this period. It's safe to water when the flower bud starts to emerge in late summer, but withhold water again from late autumn until spring, when it is safe to begin lightly watering. Don't water when the new leaves are emerging, as this will likely kill them. Wait until the old outer leaves have completely shrivelled up.

The reticulated pattern of *Lithops hookeri* makes it resemble a brain.

RECOMMENDED SPECIES

***Lithops optica* 'Rubra'**
Worth trying to find because it's a stunning milky pink-purple colour.

L. bromfieldii
Grow this one for its lovely bright-yellow flowers.

L. hookeri
The network of forked, grooved lines gives this a brain-like look.

L. dorotheae
A species with lovely distinctive red markings.

Grower profile

Tyler Thrasher

Location Tulsa, Oklahoma, United States

Specialism Mesemb cultivation, *Crassula* hybridization, *Conophytum* breeding

An author, botanist, and self-confessed "mad scientist", Tyler is fascinated by nature and has a passion for art. This combination has led to the creation of his own unique and intriguing plants.

When did you first become interested in cacti and succulents?

I grew up practically living in a greenhouse, spending most of my childhood playing and hiding among the plants. These were mostly landscaping plants, but I remember seeing my first cactus when I was around six years old. It was a prickly pear. I fell in love and began collecting my own plants in college, at around 19 years old. I haven't stopped since.

How many plants do you have in your collection?

Between mature plants, succulents, and tropicals, including seedlings, easily 2,500 to 3,000 plants.

Which plant are you most proud of and why?

That would be my *Crassula* 'Thrashula', because you can't get it anywhere else. It was the first hybrid I made – and hybridizing *Crassula* is not easy.

What's been your biggest failure, and what did you learn from that experience?

I hybridized this beautiful *Drosanthemum* I called 'Lemon Curl'. It had sparkly, curly leaves like candy – easily the coolest plant in my collection. And then we had a heatwave in Oklahoma, and it fried the entire damn plant. It was gone in a couple of hours. I'm still devastated.

How do you deal with pests?

Typically it depends on the pest. I hand-wipe most of my plants, but occasionally I will release a swarm of lacewings or ladybirds in the greenhouse.

What substrate do you use for most of your plants?

My favourite substrate is pumice. I mix pumice with a little coco coir, coarse sand, Turface clay, and a little bit of chicken grit.

Tyler holds a mature *Lithops* specimen, a recommended genus for all growers.

An as-yet-unnamed hybrid between *Crassula pubescens* and *Crassula susannae*.

Is there a common myth about growing cacti or succulents that you'd like to debunk?

Lithops species aren't hard. You just have to pay attention to their growth cycles. Same goes for most mesembs. They are some of the few succulents that have strictly defined growth cycles.

What advice would you give about watering?

Only water when the plants aren't plump. If they're turgid, leave them alone.

What advice would you give beginners?

Start slow. And start by growing from seed – why not? Be observant but don't hover over your plants. Let them grow, and pat yourself on the back for keeping them alive.

Five plants everyone should grow?

1. ***Conophytum.*** So many strange shapes and species...

2. ***Haworthia.*** Very slow-growing but rewarding after a decade or so.

3. ***Lithops.*** They flower readily and produce a lot of seed. Growing them is an entirely new learning experience.

4. ***Anacampseros.*** They're self-fertilizing and also one of the easiest plants to grow from seed.

5. ***Crassula plegmatoides.*** It's fun to say, and they're very hard to grow. Once you figure those out, you can grow any *Crassula* in the world.

What are your top tips for plant care?

Take diligent notes as you're growing. Be forgiving when you lose a plant. Sit with other growers and talk to them in person. The information you'll learn immensely outweighs what you'll read on the internet. Don't rely on the plant tag that comes with your plant. Rely on experience – your own and the experience of other growers.

Tyler's first ever hybrid, *Crassula* 'Thrashula' (top), and the dwarf succulent *Conophytum stephanii*.

Pachyphytum

Family *Crassulaceae*
Subfamily *Sempervivoideae*
Common name Moonstone, sugar almond plant, baby's fingers

The special waxy coating on the leaves of some species of *Pachyphytum* can make them look like a tasty morsel.

This is a fairly small genus containing approximately 20 species. The plants are native to Mexico, where they are often found clinging onto steep cliffs in rocky crevices at elevations of 600–1,500 metres (1,970–4,900ft) or in dry shrubland. The stems will grow upright and then droop and become prostrate, some growing to lengths in excess of 1 metre (3¼ft).

Pachyphytum leaves have a powdery-looking, waxy coating called "farina" to help protect them from the sun and aid moisture retention. This coating, combined with the pearlescent, pinky-bluish colouration of *P. oviferum* leaves, makes sense of the common name moonstone or sugar almond plant. Flowers are similar to those of *Echeveria* (see page 204), to which *Pachyphytum* is closely related, and emerge from tall, arching spikes with pretty, pendulous, greenish-white, or deep-red, bell-shaped flowers. *Pachyphytum* makes an excellent windowsill or rockery plant.

"A sweet treat"

Leaves have a powdery, waxy coating to protect them and retain moisture

Pachyphytum compactum

Pachyphytum flower petals are fused to form a tube

How to grow

Light

INDOORS On a windowsill or in a conservatory that gets direct sunlight for part of the day.
OUTSIDE Full sun or partial shade in a garden or greenhouse.

Temperature

Not cold/frost hardy. Can tolerate an average minimum temperature of 5°C (41°F).

Substrate

50% potting compost,
50% horticultural sand/grit.

Feeding

Once a month during the growing season.

Water

Allow the substrate to completely dry out between waterings. If you experience cold winters, don't water at all during this season. If you are unsure when to water, look at the lowest leaves on the stem for signs of wrinkling. This can indicate they need water. The plant is hydrated if the leaves feel firm and plump.

RECOMMENDED SPECIES

Pachyphytum viride
Leaves are fleshy and narrow, and change colour (from pale to dark green or reddish) depending on the season or environmental conditions. Petals are white, turning to lilac towards the tip.

P. rzedowskii
Soft, bluish-grey, bulbous, grape-like leaves that form a compact mound. The colour intensifies with sun exposure, turning them pinky-purple.

P. oviferum
The most popular in cultivation. Thick, pebble-shaped leaves with a pinkish tinge under intense light. Must get enough light or it will grow leggy.

Pachypodium

Family *Apocynaceae*
Subfamily *Apocynoideae*
Common name Madagascar palm, elephant's foot

A genus of succulent trees and shrubs with spiky trunks and sparse foliage that is usually concentrated at the top of the plant. They can look remarkably like palm trees, but don't be fooled.

The species of this genus are what's known as "pachycauls", meaning they grow disproportionately thick trunks for their height and bear relatively few branches. *Pachypodium lamerei* originates from the dry forests of southern and southwestern Madagascar, hence its common name of Madagascar palm, but it is not technically a palm. The deciduous leaves are long, dark green, and glossy. Spines and leaves emerge from the same node and then, as the plant matures, the leaves are slowly discarded.

Older trees often have smooth, bare trunks, with spines further up the stem and leaves only at the very top, which gives them a palm-like appearance. The flowers can be yellow, white, pink, or red, depending on the species, and make quite a beautiful display, not dissimilar to gardenia flowers. *Pachypodium* are caudiciform succulents (with a woody, water-storing stem), exhibiting a wide range of unusual growth forms, ranging in size from a few centimetres above the ground to more than 8 metres (26¼ft). Some species retain a very squat, rounded appearance, whereas others are cigar-like with a thick, shiny bark that helps reflect intense sunlight and protects them from drying out.

"Palm pretender"

Pachypodium densiflorum

A palm-like spray of elongated leaves sprouts from the top of the trunk

Spines are often arranged in whorls around the trunk

How to grow

Light

INDOORS Must be on the brightest windowsill in direct sunlight or in a conservatory. Turn the plant if it begins to lean towards the light.
OUTSIDE Full sun in a garden or greenhouse.

Temperature

Average minimum temperature of 10°C (50°F).

Substrate

25% potting compost, 75% sand/grit/pumice/perlite.

Feeding

Once or twice a year in the spring and summer growing season.

Water

Allow the substrate to completely dry out before watering. Most species lose their leaves in winter, which indicates dormancy and is your cue to stop watering as much, if at all. If growing outside, don't water if the temperature falls to 10°C (50°F).

RECOMMENDED SPECIES

Pachypodium brevicaule
The caudex is broader than it is tall and to see it in flower is a sight to behold. They make striking garden plants, especially when grouped with other caudiciforms, but are unsuitable for planting outside in cold or damp gardens.

P. lamerei
The fastest-growing and most commonly cultivated species. It is also one of the easiest to grow. A good plant for beginners.

P. rosulatum
A short, inflated base gives rise to lots of twisting branches. The flowers are on long stalks. Weirdly beautiful.

Piaranthus

Family *Apocynaceae*
Subfamily *Asclepiadoideae*

This genus has fascinatingly beautiful flowers that lure you in for a closer look, but you might need to hold your nose.

Piaranthus is a small genus of low-growing, mat-forming plants from South Africa and southern Namibia. Their stems are fleshy and vary from long and finger-like, to rounded and almost potato-shaped. Flowers emerge from the tip of the stem, often in a cluster, on elongated pedicels, from each of which one single flower will develop. The flowers are large, pretty, and unusual-looking, but beware: many species emit an unpleasant fragrance, like rancid butter or rotting vegetation, to attract flies for pollination. Flowers range in colour from white, pink, yellow, and yellowy-green to orange, red, and brown (the latter are often the most pungent). Most have very beautiful banded and dotted patterns on the petals. In bright sunlight, the stems often take on a purple-pink hue as a response to sun stress. *Piaranthus* can be grown indoors but might be reluctant to flower.

"Look but don't smell"

Stems spread over the ground in lumpen, finger-like clusters

Piaranthus globosus

The star-shaped *Piaranthus comptus* flowers are spectacular but often have an unpleasant scent.

How to grow

Light

INDOORS Position on a windowsill that receives direct sunlight.
OUTSIDE They prefer a location that avoids the intense midday sun. In a greenhouse, provide some shading.

Temperature

Average minimum temperature of 5°C (41°F) is recommended for safety, although some species can tolerate lower than this for a short period if kept dry.

Substrate

50% potting compost,
50% horticultural sand/grit.

Feeding

Once a month during the growing season.

Water

Allow the substrate to completely dry out between waterings. If you experience cold winters, don't water at all during this season.

RECOMMENDED SPECIES

Piaranthus comptus
Dark grey-green, finger-like stems with whitish flowers that have dark purple-brown spots and white conical hairs.

P. geminatus
A clumping, prostrate species that produces beautiful plump, fleshy, star-like flowers in late summer, early autumn.

P. cornutus
Globose stems with small, brilliant yellow flowers, which smell of fruit and rancid butter. Tempted?

Portulacaria

Family *Didiereaceae*
Subfamily *Portulacarioideae*
Common name Elephant bush, porkbush, purslane tree, dwarf jade

A great houseplant genus. Some species even have culinary uses. They are added to soups and salads in their native range of northwestern Kenya, Angola, South Mozambique, and South Africa.

Portulacaria currently comprises seven species, the most commonly cultivated of which is *P. afra*, which has a shrubby, branching growth habit and can grow quite large. Often confused with the jade tree (*Crassula ovata*, see page 196), *P. afra* has smaller, rounder leaves with shorter internodal spaces, giving it a more compact appearance.

Portulacaria are semi-evergreen or deciduous, depending on the species, so don't be too concerned if they drop their leaves; they will regrow as long as conditions are right. Several of the species send out clusters of small, pink flowers and are quite beautiful when in bloom. *P. pygmaea* is more understated, with small clusters of white flowers, subtly nestled among the leaves.

"Succulent soup"

Young stems are often red but develop into a greyish bark over time

Portulacaria afra

How to grow

Light

INDOORS Position on the brightest windowsill in direct sunlight or in a conservatory. They can shed their leaves as a reaction to low light levels.
OUTSIDE Full sun or partial shade in a garden or greenhouse.

Temperature

Average minimum temperature of 5°C (41°F) is recommended for safety, although some species can tolerate lower than this for a short period if kept dry.

Substrate

50% potting compost, 50% sand/grit/pumice/perlite.

Feeding

Once a month during the spring and summer growing season.

Water

Allow the substrate to completely dry out before watering. Winter dormancy can be induced by low light levels. If this happens, stop or reduce watering dramatically until brighter, longer days return.

RECOMMENDED SPECIES

Portulacaria pygmaea
These make great bonsai plants due to their thick stems and roots.

P. namaquensis
Very unique in appearance. Has a woody stem with very small, semi-deciduous, ovate leaves. Usually grown in cultivation grafted onto the stem of *P. afra*.

P. afra
A popular evergreen shrub, which makes a great houseplant. Also used for bonsai. There is also *P. afra* 'Variegata', with attractive reddish-brown stems and smooth, glossy green leaves with cream-coloured margins.

Raphionacme

Family *Apocynaceae*
Subfamily *Periplocoideae*
Common name Milkplant root

All *Raphionacme* species grow underground tubers, most of which are large and bulb-like. Potting them so the tuber or caudex is above ground makes a very different and intriguing-looking plant.

These are caudiciform plants, primarily found in Africa, with a swollen, woody, stem-like storage organ. If you were to look for *Raphionacme* plants in their habitat at the wrong time of year (during autumn and winter when they are dormant), you would have great difficulty finding any, as only a small proportion of the plant is visible above ground, and they only produce vines and leaves during the growing season. These vines can reach 1–2 metres (3¼–6½ft) in length, so it's advisable to have a small trellis for them to climb up.

I fell in love with a *R. burkei* (pictured here) while visiting the London plant shop Conservatory Archives (see page 154). While it may resemble a flatbread to some, this squashed turnip-shaped caudex, usually hidden underground, is the survival organ of the plant, storing water and nutrients that can be utilized when rainfall is scarce. Of the 30 or so *Raphionacme* species, many are now threatened or thought to be already extinct in the wild due to habitat loss, climate change, and poaching. The caudex is used for hydration and nutrition by the Khoisan hunter-gatherer populations of Namibia, Botswana, and South Africa.

"Underground, overground"

Raphionacme burkei

How to grow

Light

INDOORS Needs direct sunlight when growing, on the brightest windowsill or in a conservatory. **OUTSIDE** The leaves like direct sunlight but the caudex prefers to be shaded. When the plant is dormant, make sure the caudex isn't in direct sunlight.

The caudex of some species is round and squashed like a flatbread

Temperature

Average minimum temperature of 10°C (50°F) is recommended for safety, although some species can tolerate lower than this for a short period if kept dry.

Substrate

80% grit/sand/pumice,
20% potting compost.

Feeding

Once a month only when growing (i.e. when there are leaves on the plant).

Water

When growing they tend to need a lot of water. Check the substrate regularly during the growing season and water as soon as it becomes dry. Try not to get water on the caudex to reduce the risk of rot. Don't water when dormant. As a rule: NO vine = NO water.

RECOMMENDED SPECIES

Raphionacme flanaganii
A relatively fast-growing and hardy species. Grows dark-green, slightly glossy leaves with fuzzy undersides, and small, sweet-smelling flowers in summer.

R. burkei
Has a beautiful, large, spherical, flattened caudex, which has a smooth surface and is light beige in colour.

Sedum pachyphyllum

Sedum

Family *Crassulaceae*
Subfamily *Sempervivoideae*
Common name Stonecrop, burro's tail, donkey tail, miniature Joshua tree, jelly beans

"Spoilt for choice"

This genus is so diverse it is almost impossible to describe it by physical appearance in a concise manner. Fast-growing, beautifully coloured, and hardy are three phrases that best sum up its many species.

Sedum plants are found primarily in the northern hemisphere but extend into the southern hemisphere in Africa and South America. One of the most popular and recognizable of the 400–500 species is *S. morganianum*, known as burro's or donkey tail, which has pendulous, fleshy stems, densely covered with pale bluish-green succulent leaves that set off the red flowers beautifully. A great example of the physical diversity within this genus is another popular species, *S. multiceps*, which couldn't look more different. This plant has a more upright growth pattern and takes on the appearance of a miniature tree, giving it one of its common names, the miniature Joshua tree. Several other species, such as *S. reflexum* and *S. spurium*, are popular choices for outdoor ground cover, owing to their hardiness and creeping growth patterns. Indoors, outdoors, window boxes, pots, roofs, retaining walls, or rockeries – there is a *Sedum* plant suitable for almost every environment.

Sedum morganianum can be easily propagated from a single leaf.

How to grow

Light

INDOORS *Sedum morganianum* needs to be close to a window that receives direct sunlight only in the morning or late afternoon. They don't like direct sunlight all day. Provide shade from the midday/afternoon sun in a conservatory.
OUTSIDE Most grow best in full sun, apart from *S. morganianum*, which prefers shade from the midday sun.

Temperature

Many species can tolerate temperatures below freezing, while others, such as *S. morganianum*, prefer a minimum of 5°C (41°F).

Substrate

50% potting compost, 50% horticultural sand/grit/perlite.

Feeding

Once a month when growing indoors. Not necessary if planted in the garden.

Water

If growing indoors, allow the soil to dry out completely between waterings. Keep dry if winter days are short and cold.

RECOMMENDED SPECIES

Sedum morganianum
Large examples are extremely impressive. Best grown in situ with minimal disturbance as the leaves fall off very easily. If this happens, simply drop them back into the top of the pot where they will root.

S. pachyphyllum
Leaves resemble jelly beans, hence another common name. They are a glossy green colour with red tints under strong light.

S. oxypetalum
A small tree-shaped shrub, which can be grown as bonsai-type tree.

Sempervivum

Family *Crassulaceae*
Subfamily *Sempervivoideae*
Common name Houseleek, hen and chicks, liveforever

These low-growing rosettes are often confused for *Echeveria*

***Sempervivum* (mix)**

"I think the house has a leek"

Sempervivum 'Pink Lotus' forms a tight rosette and green and pink.

In Anglo-Saxon times *Sempervivum* was planted onto thatched roofs to protect them from fire and lightning strikes. The common name of houseleek is derived from the Anglo-Saxon word leac, a plant, so houseleek literally means "the house plant".

Sempervivum is a genus of rosette-forming succulents that spread by sending out stolons (runners) from the base of the plant, which grow a single new rosette at the tip that roots into the ground. They are monocarpic, so the rosette from which the flower stem emerges will die once the flowers have gone to seed. There are around 40 species and thousands of cultivars with a wide range of rosette sizes, forms, and colours.

Often confused with other rosette-forming succulents, such as *Echeveria* (see page 204), *Sempervivum* can be recognized by their thinner, less succulent leaves and the stolons where offsets form. Originating in mountain habitats across Europe, Morocco, and western Asia, where they grow on rocky outcrops, they are a common choice for garden ground cover and rockeries as they are very resilient, capable of withstanding heavy rainfall, full sun, very low temperatures, and snow.

How to grow

Light

OUTSIDE Not suitable for indoor growing, unless under a grow light. Plant them in full sun in the garden.

Temperature

Most are cold-hardy and can tolerate temperatures well below 0°C (32°F) but they must be in free-draining substrate otherwise they can rot in cold temperatures.

Substrate

Free-draining soil with added sand and grit. Dislikes overly fertile soil and areas prone to water retention.

Feeding

Not necessary.

Water

Some prefer to be sheltered from excessive rain in winter. The trichomes of some of the "hairy" species hold moisture around the leaves. This can cause them to rot in winter, so plant where they get enough winter sun to dry out.

RECOMMENDED SPECIES

Sempervivum arachnoideum
Has cobweb-like trichomes, which join together to resemble spider webs across the rosettes.

S. calcareum
The leaves are mostly blue-green and have intensely red tips. Prefers lime-free soil.

***S.* 'Red Beauty'**
Larger rosettes of light-green leaves that have a maroon tint as the temperature drops. The pink star-shaped flowers appear in late summer.

Stapelia

Family *Apocynaceae*
Subfamily *Asclepiadoideae*
Common name Carrion flower, African starfish flowers

The angular, finger-like stems and remarkable flowers make this one of my all-time favourite succulents. I would collect every species and fill my greenhouse with them were it not for the horrendous smell most emit when they bloom.

Please don't let the stink put you off growing them; *Stapelia* species truly are a wonder of nature. The putrid odour of rotting meat explains their common name carrion flowers and is a clever ploy to attract flies. Drawn to the smell, the flies move around the flower, searching for places to lay eggs, and in the process are dusted with pollen, which they carry to the next flower.

Stapelia are native to southeastern Africa, where they can form large clumps up to 2 metres (6½ft) across, bearing fleshy flowers that range in colour from red, to purple, or yellow, often with the most incredible patterns, and some are hairy. They often grow in the shade of other plants or in rocky crevices, so that there is some natural filtering of the high light intensity. Hence why they need some protection from the strongest sunlight.

"A big stink"

Stapelia variegata

How to grow

Light

INDOORS A bright windowsill that receives a few hours of direct sunlight.
OUTSIDE A location that avoids intense midday sun. Provide some shading in a greenhouse.

Temperature

No lower than about 8–10°C (46–50°F). Plants can be brought inside for the winter and placed near a window.

Stapelia clumps can reach almost 1 metre (3ft) in diameter

Stapelia leendertziae f. *cristata* has unusual wave-like crested stems.

Substrate

50% horticultural sand/grit, 50% potting compost. Add a layer of grit on the soil surface to prevent moisture from accumulating around the base of the stems.

Feeding

Once a month during the growing season.

Water

Stapelia are prone to disintegrate into a heap of rotten stems if given too much water, or watered once the temperature drops below 10°C (50°F). Do not water at all in cold winters. At all other times, allow to completely dry out between watering.

RECOMMENDED SPECIES

Stapelia gigantea
Spectacularly large, stunningly beautiful flowers that come in a variety of colours.

S. leendertziae* f. *cristata
The big balloon-shaped, dark red to purple flowers are awe-inspiring – just don't get too close.

Yucca

Family *Asparagaceae*
Subfamily *Agavoideae*
Common name Spanish bayonet, Spanish dagger, Adam's needle and thread, bear-grass, needle-palm

Whether you're looking for an easy-care houseplant or a sculptural statement in the garden, this genus has got you covered.

Native to the Americas and the Caribbean, *Yucca* is remarkably varied and diverse, with 49 species found in a wide range of habitats, from humid rainforests and wet subtropical ecosystems to hot, dry deserts. Most *Yucca* are terrestrial apart from one unusual species: *Y. lacandonica*, which is an epiphyte and grows primarily on trees in tropical dry forests.

Though they vary greatly in appearance, with some being almost stemless and quite compact while others reach impressive heights, generally *Yucca* plants are known for their sword-like leaves, which give them the architectural appearance that have made them so popular both in the home and outside. The white or similarly pale flowers are extremely striking, adding to their popularity as statement garden plants. Iconic species include *Y. brevifolia*, commonly known as the Joshua tree. *Yucca* are pollinated by yucca moths, which play a vital role in the plants' survival. Without the yucca moth, the plant would lose its only pollinator, and without the plant, the moth would lose its food source. Each depends on the other for survival.

"Making a point"

Yucca gigantea

Some species have tough, spiky leaves while others are softer

How to grow

Light

INDOORS The ubiquitous *Y. gigantea* (syn. *Y. elephantipes*) can tolerate lower light intensities but needs to be near a bright window to thrive. **OUTSIDE** *Yucca* can be planted in full sun or semi-shade.

Temperature

Some species can tolerate below freezing temperatures if kept dry, while others, such as *Y. elephantipes*, are best kept above 5°C (41°F).

Substrate

50% potting compost, 50% horticultural sand/grit/perlite.

Feeding

Once a month during the growing season.

Water

If growing indoors, allow the substrate to dry out between waterings. Reduce watering during the cold winter months.

RECOMMENDED SPECIES

***Yucca gigantea* (syn. *Y. elephantipes*)**
Often referred to simply as yucca cane or cane yucca. A very easy-going houseplant if positioned close to a bright window and only watered when the substrate is completely dry. Remember, they are a succulent!

Y. filamentosa
A compact, hardy species with striking sword-like leaves and dramatic flowerheads. Makes a great focal point in a garden.

Y. rostrata
Has a dramatic trunk and beautiful thin blue leaves that create a perfectly round orb.

Grower profile

Santino Rischitelli

Location Melbourne, Australia

Specialism Growing outside

Membership Cactus and Succulent Society of Australia (CSSA)

Santino has been collecting and growing cacti and succulents in his garden in Australia for decades. He's a keen propagator and sells his home-grown plants at the local market, where he enjoys sharing his knowledge with customers.

Santino's *Echinopsis pachanoi* (syn. *Trichocereus pachanoi*) and *Aloe plicatilis* form the main features of a striking display.

Which plant in your collection are you most proud of and why?

My *Crassula perfoliata* var. *heterotricha*. I think this may be my favourite plant. When I received it, it was only small. However, within a few months it had grown substantially and flowered already, despite being young. I love the colours in the leaves.

What's been your biggest failure, and what did you learn from that experience?

I learnt the hard way that when you buy plants you should not put them among your collection straight away. Keep them in quarantine for a few weeks, away from your other plants, to ensure they don't introduce any nasties to your collection, like mealybugs.

What substrate do you use for most of your plants?

Where I live in Melbourne, the soil is very sandy. When I first started collecting I used soil from my garden. However, now I buy topsoil from a nursery, which I mix with three types of potting mix and pebbles. I use this for all my plants.

What advice would you give beginners?

When starting a collection, I advise learning the plant names if you can. As your collection grows you don't want to keep buying plants you already have. If possible, you want to understand the original growing environment of your plants. Some nurseries grow plants in greenhouses, then people purchase them, bring them home, put them in full sun and burn the plants.

Five plants everyone should grow and why?

1. *Crassula perfoliata* var. *minor* (*falcata*). Very easy to grow in morning sun or full sun. They have beautiful red flowers yearly and a nice scent.

2. *Sedum adolphi.* A very sun-tolerant plant and quite hardy, with beautiful white flowers.

3. *Gymnocalycium*. Small, clump-forming plants, which don't grow too large.

4. *Echinopsis oxygona.* Easy cactus plants to grow. They produce lots of offsets, which can be removed to make new plants. The larger they are, the more flowers they have.

5. *Echeveria elegans.* Can be grown in morning sun to full sun quite happily. They produce many offsets and form a nice clump within a short period of time, and have lovely multicoloured flowers.

What are your top tips for plant care?

Learn about the genus of a plant to understand its basic requirements, if not specific species requirements. Get to know each plant so you notice any changes early. Share information about your plants and learn from fellow collectors.

The ripple jade plant, *Crassula arborescens* subsp. *undulatifolia* (top); succulent *Cotyledon papillaris* (middle); *Aloe juvenna*, or tiger tooth aloe (bottom).

Index

The plant profile page reference for genera is in bold.

R

S

T

U

V

W

X

Y

Z

Acknowledgements

Author's acknowledgements

This book exists because of the love and support of my husband James and daughter Eva who put up with living with way too many plants and have braved the injuries from hefting countless cacti in and out of the house with unwavering patience. To my mum and dad, thank you for gifting me the space and time of a writing retreat and for always nurturing my creativity. Much love to my brother, Ewan, and his wife, Adele, for providing room in their house for the overflow of plants.

To all my friends, thank you for being my sounding board, sharing my passion, and enduring endless musings about plants. A special thank you to the British Cactus and Succulent Society and its dedicated members, especially Graham Charles, whose knowledge has been invaluable, and to Julian Cooke, Steph Wilson, Mellie Lewis, Paul Spraklin, and Ian Woolnough for the tour of your wonderful homes, gardens, and greenhouses.

A huge thanks to the fantastic team at DK, my agent Clare Hulton, and to Jason Ingram, whose incredible photography has brought the beauty of these plants to life.

And finally, my gratitude to Jin from Conservatory Archives (conservatoryarchives.co.uk) and Hayley from Mint Plants (mintplants.co.uk) for generously allowing us to capture shots within your beautiful premises. This book wouldn't be the same without the spirit and support of everyone mentioned here—thank you all for helping make it a reality.

Publisher's acknowledgements

Dorling Kindersley would like to thank everyone at West Dean Gardens and especially Head Gardener Tom Brown for granting access to photograph the collection of succulents. Thanks also to Adam Brackenbury and Sunil Sharma for repro work, Kathy Steer for proofreading, and Ruth Ellis for indexing.

Picture credits

The publisher would like to thank the following for their kind permission to reproduce their photographs:

(Key: a-above; b-below/bottom; c-centre; f-far; l-left; r-right; t-top)

15 naturepl.com: Barrie Britton (bl). **20-21 Alamy Stock Photo:** Delphine Adburgham (t). **20 Shutterstock.com:** Raul Luna (bl). **22-23 Alamy Stock Photo:** Florapix (c). **24-25 Shutterstock.com:** WillieBez (b). **26 Alamy Stock Photo:** Gary Cook (br). **28 Alamy Stock Photo:** Sunpix Travel (cr). **29 Alamy Stock Photo:** Larry Geddis (b). **30 Alamy Stock Photo:** Peter Horree (tl); Jorge Tutor (tr). **31 Alamy Stock Photo:** David Moore (b). **33 Alamy Stock Photo:** blickwinkel. **42 Luke Ricketts:** (clb). **43 Luke Ricketts:** (tl). **68-69 Sara Blanchard:** (c). **93 Sara Blanchard:** (br). **110-111 Adobe Stock:** Oleg Kovtun (bc). **111 Getty Images:** Paul Starosta (tr). **112 Alamy Stock Photo:** Patricia Weston (c). **113 Alamy Stock Photo:** Bob Gibbons (c). **115 Alamy Stock Photo: Florapix** (tr). **120 Graham Charles:** (b). **121 Graham Charles:** (tc). **123 Getty Images:** Stone / Ed Reschke (tr). **136 Edgar Vargas:** (bl). **137 Edgar Vargas:** (tl, br). **138-139 Alamy Stock Photo:** Hazrat Bilal (b). **142-143 Shutterstock.com:** Andrey Zheludev (b). **163 Dreamstime.com:** Rob Lumen Captum (bc). **164 SuperStock:** Eye Ubiquitous. **168 James Gerrard-Jones:** (tr, bl). **169 James Gerrard-Jones:** (br). **176-177 Adobe Stock:** luckypic. **183 James Gerrard-Jones:** (tl, tr, bl, br). **194 Ferah and Glen:** (bl). **195 Ferah and Glen:** (tr, bl). **198-199 Ferah and Glen:** (c). **199 Ferah and Glen:** (br). **210 Lyn Kimberley:** (b). **211 Lyn Kimberley:** (crb, br). **219 Getty Images / iStock:** E+ / Sproetniek (tr). **226 Tyler Thrasher:** (br). **227 Tyler Thrasher:** (tl, crb, br). **233 Alamy Stock Photo:** imageBROKER / Erich Geduldig (t). **246 Santino Rischitelli:** (br). **247 Santino Rischitelli:** (tr, tc, br)

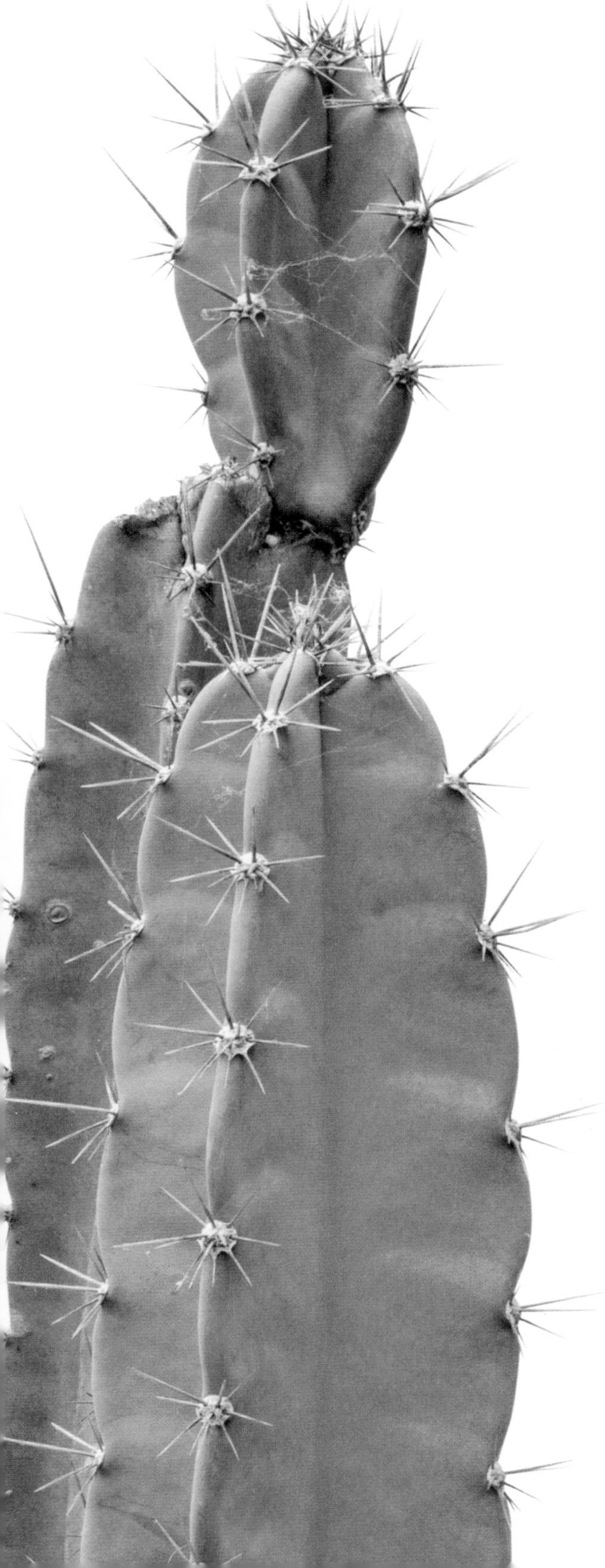

Senior Editor Alastair Laing
Senior Designer Barbara Zuniga
Design Assistant Izzy Poulson
Publishing Assistant Emily Cannings
DTP and Design Coordinator Heather Blagden
Senior Picture Researcher Aditya Katyal
Production Editor David Almond
Production Controller Kariss Ainsworth
Art Director Maxine Pedliham
Editorial Manager Ruth O'Rourke

Editorial Holly Kyte
Design Christine Keilty, Nikki Ellis
Photography Jason Ingram
Illustration Stuart Jackson-Carter

First published in Great Britain in 2025 by
Dorling Kindersley Limited
20 Vauxhall Bridge Road,
London SW1V 2SA

The authorised representative in the EEA is
Dorling Kindersley Verlag GmbH. Arnulfstr. 124,
80636 Munich, Germany

10 9 8 7 6 5 4 3 2 1
001–342956–Apr/2025

A CIP catalogue record for this book
is available from the British Library.
ISBN: 978-0-2416-9589-0

Printed and bound in China
www.dk.com

This book was made with Forest Stewardship Council™ certified paper – one small step in DK's commitment to a sustainable future.
Learn more at **www.dk.com/uk/information/sustainability**

About the author

Sarah Gerrard-Jones, author of *The Plant Rescuer*, is a self-taught plant obsessive with a passion for rescuing ailing houseplants and a particular interest in cacti and succulents. As @theplantrescuer on Instagram, Sarah has helped thousands of people understand how to make their plants happy and what to do if something goes wrong. She is a natural communicator and ardently believes in making plants, and their care, accessible to everyone.

Sarah is a presenter on ITV's Alan Titchmarsh's Gardening Club and has been featured on BBC Gardeners' World. She writes for BBC Gardeners' World Magazine, The Sunday Times and Gardens Illustrated and won a Gold Medal at RHS Chelsea Flower Show.